# Give yourself™ a brand

WITH A STRONG FOUNDATION
AND MAKE THE WORLD
A BETTER PLACE

**Learn more at:**
**giveyourselfabrand.com**

2nd Edition published in 2024 by Claptrap Press
First published in 2019 by Claptrap Press



Claptrap Press
www.claptrappress.com

ISBN 978-1-9160170-9-2 (Paperback)

A CIP catalogue record for this book is available from the British Library.

*Here's to those who dare to keep trying.*

**Branding is a profound manifestation of the human condition.**

*Wally Olins*

**You get in life what you have the courage to ask for.**

*Oprah Winfrey*

**I think it's wrong that only one company makes the game Monopoly.**

*Steven Wright*

# Give yourself™ a brand

WITH A STRONG FOUNDATION
AND MAKE THE WORLD
A BETTER PLACE

**Luke Arwen Shaw**

# Contents

# Hello

Branding. I know, it's not a new concept. But it *is* an effective one and remains a rich means of attaining success. So, if you wish to find your unique value and share it with the world in exchange for true remuneration, you've come to the right place.

I will start by saying:

I don't know you.

Or what you love doing.

Or what your strengths are.

I don't know what your comparative advantage is, what you do for a job, or how you like to engage with the world.

But *you* do.

And if you don't, you soon will.

And when you combine that self-knowledge with the knowledge you're going to get from this book, you are going to be unstoppable.

In the following chapters, I'm going to share everything I know about branding and lay down a simple process that will enable you to conceptualise, package, and sell your value via your very own brand.

A brand you can grow, be proud of, and employ, to make better use of your unique talents, so you can be all that you can be, live your best life, achieve Peak Fun, and make your soul sing with joy. Which, by the way, is a good thing to do.

(NB: In some places, I am going to take common nouns and make them look like proper nouns. For example, I might write Activity with a big A, here and there. Please allow me this one small indulgence. I will *try* to do this sparingly but in some cases, for example, when unpacking an acronym, I'm sure it will aid understanding. No need to thank me.)

So, you still want to give yourself a brand?
In *this* economy?
Take a seat, dear reader. We've got work to do.

You see, it's never been easier to connect with people via socials. Never been easier to dance in front of a phone and win fifty thousand likes. Never been easier to pump every orifice of the internet with more content than it knows what to do with. And it's never been easier to think you're achieving success, or failure, by counting your followers. But if you're serious about sharing your unique value with the world in exchange for truer remuneration, that needs to stop. We need to rethink your entire approach. Go *outside* the box, if you will.

And we initiate that by counting our blessings.

Firstly, you're amazing. And no, I don't say that to just anyone.

Secondly, you're a human. Social, conscious, and creative, with access to a powerful mind, living in a wonderful universe that wants to help you achieve your dreams.

Thirdly, I slap you hard across the jowls like the fool you are and scold your naivety. This is planet Earth, mate. A complex, fast-moving, hostile-rich environment. Things are tricky and difficult and it's hard to be all that you can be, and live your best life, achieve Peak Fun, and make your soul sing with joy.

But you know that ... it's why you've stayed in your lane all these years, toiling under the illusion of progress, binging carbs and boxsets, living up to the expectations of others ... it's what, well, what life expects.

'Your time is limited,' announced Steve Jobs, during his commencement address at Stanford University, 'so don't waste it living someone else's life.'

Good advice, Steve, but almost impossible to pull off.

People may have hidden value, unique experience, untapped wells of tremendous potential and the mind to see a particular constellation that no one else sees but it takes time and money to get that value wrestled into something saleable. In most cases success requires failure, and few of us have the resources to bankroll endless experiment.

We have mouths to feed. And bills to pay. And you can't pay the rent with some half-baked idea of how you might make loungewear from bubble wrap.

So you work in sales, or tech support, or marketing.

But somewhere in your fevered daydreams could be the creation of a super brand—slicker than Apple, smoother than Porsche, chai lattier than Starbucks.

Somewhere in your intelligent imagination lies a vision.

Maybe it looks misty and vague, or maybe it's sharp and clear, but I'll bet it appears over a seemingly long and impossible road.

Well ... the journey towards anything worthwhile is always difficult.

And this is the best opportunity you've ever had. It's not perfect, but it's available. As a social, conscious being in a limitless mind, on an oxygen-rich planet where humanity does its business, waist-deep in bubble wrap, endangered sea life, and hotdog packets, searching for meaning and validation and Wi-Fi.

When else, and where else, are you going to have such a good chance of developing your amazing ideas? If not here, where? If not now, when?

So go back to that napkin or newspaper or notebook and reclaim your idea. And then...

You will encounter three problems.

Your first problem will be one of Motivation.

'Shall I? Shall I not?'

This is the idea bouncing in your head like a Swingball. You're a reasonable person and so your mind reasons. Flits the idea like a confused Alsatian with an unusual biscuit. 'Idea good? Or bad? You cross-examine both cases, defence and prosecution, FOR and AGAINST, pacing up and down in doubt and belief.

Ideas can "swingball" in a human head for years, but they only get acted upon for three reasons: love, desperation, or [other].

It doesn't really matter which one applies to you, because in this life, success comes, if it ever does, from either perseverance, luck, or some combination of the two.

But swingball the idea you will, for a while, and this is good. But at some point, your idea will need to see some action.

'Ok,' you think, 'I'll act upon my idea but first I'll just check that everyone in my wide group of family, friends, and business acquaintances, is ok with this.'

Problem Number Two. The desire to attain blanket Approval.

Now, I should say here that it can of course be valuable to get advice and feedback from other people. This book isn't our "special little secret" ... I'm not trying to groom you. Sure, get feedback. Without it vulnerable people can get miked up and ushered onto well-lit stages only to find their fevered dreams of pop success broken by a baying audience and Simon C, at the neon desk of judgment, frowning, as he corrects yet another lost soul with black-jerseyed shrugs of brutal feedback and counsel.

We all learn eventually.

So, by all means, accelerate the process. By all means, seek feedback and counsel ... but take only that which resonates. And the voice you must give the greatest attention to is the quiet still one that sits inside your innermost self.

So, close social media for a minute.

Step away from the pizza gangbang emoji.

If we're going to seriously give you a brand, if we're going to clean up the oceans and clean up the kitchen and create things worth creating, we need to ditch your need for external validation and start doing things *your* way. We need to de-flatter you until you can stand in your own skin and last five minutes without an empty symbol of digital encouragement.

Let it go. Breathe.

Give yourself Approval.

The third and final problem will be one of Patience.

Once people decide to act upon a goal they are filled with energy and motivation. But that energy and motivation does not last long amid the constant distraction and upset of everyday life. Spelling mistakes, rail cancellations, sore throats, power cuts. Every day blocked drains, inconsiderate drivers, out-of-order engraving machines in your local pet store, 'The nearest engraving store is a ten-mile drive!'

This ceaseless drudge-a-thon makes it hard to hunt down your dreams and be your best you. Makes it hard to get confident and dynamic and dressed for success in tight white denim like an unexploded sex bomb.

Very hard ... you have to be patient.

Ok, so you fell in love with your idea. It seduced your brains out and got you pregnant and led you up the aisle but honeymoons end. Fast.

Your idea *will* come to bore and displease you. As you progress, you'll see its flaws and shortcomings and the hard work needed to make it all it can be. You'll need to be patient and work hard with the idea.

Care for the idea.

Make it sandwiches and cups of tea.

And the long, drawn-out, phases of devotion required can sap the best of us.

Your mind is your best friend but it can be your worst enemy. You must stay vigilant. Learning is made of failure, but that failure can destroy you if you're not careful.

Reframe "failure" and find the lessons you can use to move forward. Reframe as fast as possible. Patience keeps your mind on course and helps you sleep and enthusiasm will always return to pick you up the next morning.

So, yes, you have started on your way to giving yourself a brand and making your best self happen, but it's essential you also give yourself...

- Motivation
- Approval
- Patience

I like to call these three initial bullets: "The MAP". And this three-letter acronym is undeniable. It will never change. Three nouns of power. Treasure the wisdom they bestow and you'll need little more.

The above rambling is, of course, the intro section... the entree ... the palate-cleansing sorbet of general life coaching cardio to tee you up and get you in the zone, but now, listen hard, 'cos things are about to get technical.

The first thing you need to know is that branding is all just an A.C.T.

Yes, it's an acronym: A.C.T. stands for Abilities, Content, and Touchpoints.

**Abilities** are the value-creating things a brand can actually do.

These are quite important. By which I mean vital.

Abilities determine the goods and services a brand can offer and determine to what extent it can transform end-users.

For example, the principal Abilities of the Apple brand are the design and production of incredible technology products such as Macbooks, iPhones, and iPads. Porsche's Abilities are the design and production of high-performance sports cars. And Starbucks provides coffee and European-style cafe experiences to its end-users.

Abilities are what you can do.

If you are not able to do it, you can't offer it. But if you can do it, you can do it, and more importantly, you can brand it.

It's good to know what your Abilities are when venturing out to provide value but if you're still working out exactly where you transform people, or where you can package up Ability as part of a brand, then now is the perfect time to do that. Always better to reflect upon fundamentals at the beginning of a new project than halfway through. It saves time and money.

The process laid out in this book will help you whether you know your Abilities or not. And the following chapters can even serve as a useful means of helping you define and develop your Abilities. Now, obviously I cannot provide specific advice on your specific Abilities because I am not an all-knowing God, however as we progress there will be plenty of junctures, I assure you, for you to see new opportunities or stress-test any assumptions you had about where you can provide value.

But one thing is clear, giving yourself a brand can elevate your Abilities and transform the way you provide value to others. Which of course is a powerful key to personal success.

(NB: You'll notice above I cracked open a can of "Proper Noun" for abilities/Abilities. Why? Because you're worth it.)

<u>**Content** is everything a brand knows and can share with its audiences.</u>

For example, the words, pictures, videos, or diagrams, on a brand's website.

"Content."

It's a word. A concept. A concept that divides people (like QR codes) but ultimately it's just communication, really. Communicating with your tribe.

Humans are information-sharing animals and, in the art of selling your goods and services, it is vital that your goods and services are known about, talked about, and used.

And that's where Content comes in.

No matter what form it may take, from adverts to articles, demos to activations, podcasts to product placement, or a PR event featuring holographic orangutans, it is vital that your brand generates Content that your audiences can find you through, and become stuck in, as they surely fall for your inimitable charms.

Content is a very effective "Signposting"* activity that will direct your end-users towards your actual offering. It will inform people what your brand actually does. And everyone will be better guided towards using your goods and services.

However, [looks around to check for eavesdroppers] Content can also talk about, or show, related subject matter.

'What?' you scream, 'related subject matter?'

Yes, you can show helpful materials from third parties that your end-users can use, and learn from, without any obvious connection to your goods and services. I know, pretty mad. And this can help to win trust and credibility and build a community around your brand.

Content can be dismissed by the cool kids but there's no getting away from it, Content rules.

(NB: FYI: BTW: The above is not necessarily about 'Content Marketing', which is kind of its own thing. Obviously, Content Marketing is all about Content and very "adjacent" but maybe lower the volume on the **M** word for a bit because, hey, kids, everything is **M**arketing of some kind.)

* See page 223.

**Touchpoints** are simply the points where a brand touches its audiences.

The key touchpoints of Apple are its products, and for Starbucks, it will be the coffee, the cups, and the cafe interiors.

Touchpoints can be anything really—a website, an advert, a branded umbrella, or an event like a race day at the Porsche headquarters—it all depends on the exact nature of the brand you wish to create.

A touchpoint is every single place someone is touched by your brand.

Your receptionist's smile, your signage, your email newsletters, your telephonist's voice and manner, your handshake, your walk.

Everything that 'touches' your end-user. Although always be careful about actually touching your end-users with your hand, or other body parts, as that can cause legal issues. In fact, many of your Touchpoints do have the power to cause negative outcomes, so it really is always worth giving deep consideration to each and every one. A Touchpoint can win a new fan but can also turn someone off.

Not every last aspect of your brand's interplay with the world can be designed and managed from cradle to grave—some things will just be unintended consequences, like for example a wrapper from one of your donuts being dropped, or wind-whisked, into someone's front garden. But the "Art of Life" is seeing which parts we should try to control, and your brand's Touchpoints are one such part.

And so any time you *do* invest, it should be a wise and reasoned use of resources. Relevant and meaningful.

It should mean something. To someone.

Just because you can stick your logo on 5000 pens doesn't mean you *should*. (Although, people do always need a pen.)

How your brand touches its audience will largely determine its success or failure—and the means you use to do that will be driven, shaped, and limited by your planning, your resources, your circumstances, and your imagination.

If you're a manufacturer of high-performance sports cars you'll touch your audience not with hands or other body parts but with the visceral beauty of your end product, the weight of your key fob, the plushness of your upholstery, and /or the stunning photographs of your curvaceous range. A computer hardware manufacturer will touch end-users via the quality of its devices, the ergonomic design of its keyboards, and/or the elegance of its advertising spots. A high street optician will touch by means of eye testing, lens cloths, and spectacles. A musician will use music, videos, poems, and posters.

And all will use social media, a very effective part of one's brand and marketing mix.

Social media platforms—such as Instagram, X (formerly Twitter), YouTube, and LinkedIn—are, of course, very powerful platforms and tools that provide endless scrollable joy to millions. They are terrific Touchpoints between brands and their audiences *but* it is worth remembering they are isolated platforms and tools. And for them to truly leverage the power of your brand and what that all means to your audience, they will need to connect to a greater platform. And that greater platform is your brand's foundation.

Branding is all just an A.C.T. but before a brand *can* A.C.T., it first needs a foundation on which to perform.

But worry not, because the next few chapters will provide you with one. Grab a sandwich and some comestibles, perhaps an oatmilk latté, and hoover up my eight simple easy-to-follow steps. Yes, this does make me sound like an online fitness instructor but hey, maybe that's how I should approach this: I'm your personal trainer.

So, let's get into it. Let's knock some reps out.

It's not going to be pretty, or easy, or pretty easy.

But it will be worth it.

And once you have your brand's foundation you can then A.C.T.

You can ACT out a brilliant performance—truly authentic to you and your tribe.

This is your opportunity to take back what you love, what you know, and what you're good at. To leverage all that latent power and package it all up.

Yes, I know branding is a shady anti-human practice used by immoral corporate overlords to leech money from good people. Of course, it is, but this is your opportunity to learn some of those immoral corporate overlord tricks, so you can make more money, set up a charity for injured cocker spaniels, and become a fair-playing spaniel-loving overlord. And if there's one thing we all need right now it's fair-playing spaniel-loving overlords.

So do it. And do it now, on planet Earth in the 21st Century. Because this is your time.

Yes, our current historical moment is rife with confusion, hatred, fear, and injustice. Yes, we have to accept cookies every five minutes. And yes, there is shame, anger, and the fast pace of technological change. The human experience is jam-packed with things to depress us. But it always was. Existence is problematic. Life is visceral and concise. We are defeatist and elitist, populist, and poorly educated. We differ in opinion. We're afflicted by the second law of thermodynamics, intellectual myopia, homicide, insomnia, climate change, collective delusions, the widely held misconception of limited resources, negative emotional states, misuse of pillows, microplastics, a propensity to dehumanise others, gravity, uncertainty, accidental death, storm damage, cancer, confusion, status anxiety, corrupt systems of governance, drones and the threat of all-out robot war.

But look on the bright side, fortunately, we also have consciousness, infinite creativity, intelligent debate, the concept of fair play, gravity, uncertainty, comedy, checks and balances, social cohesion, proper use of pillows, positive emotional states, a tendency to help strangers, the capacity to develop resistance to stress through the intelligent reframing of one's viewpoints, sex, ever-growing access to a broad spectrum of opinion and specialist expertise, the development and distribution of life-saving medicines, yoga, well-negotiated arbitration between power-brokers, peace in our time, facilitators, wedding discos, drive-thru restaurants, drones and the ability to get stunning aerial footage for the price of a city break.

So we have a choice. We can let our fear excuse us from action, or we can repurpose the energy of those fears into faith, educate ourselves into development, and ship the best version of ourselves yet.

Whichever route you choose, you can make happen, but the overriding purpose of this book is to help you focus on the stuff that matters to you. So you can develop that into a brand—the ultimate tool for leveraging the stuff that matters.

Branding is a practice. It is an art. It is a discipline. A science. A trade. It is also many other things which I will explain in a bit. But it's really just about expression, about bridging your inner world with the outer world.

You may be a couch potato school-leaver glued to a computer game or a nonagenarian marathon runner. You may believe in pre-determined fate or random free will. You may be a freelance health inspector, you may work in sales. You may be Head of Marketing for an international conglomerate. You may be a small business, a big business, a sole agent, or a lottery-funded canoe club for ex-servicemen.

It doesn't matter ... the only thing to remember is what Shakespeare said, 'Above all else, to thine own self be true.'

So let's be true to ourselves, let's forget everyone else. Forget the boss, forget the neighbours, and forget the trolls.

'What trolls?'

Exactly.

Embrace your ideas and put them somewhere safe, within view, and read this book and pretty soon you'll have a brand of your very own. A brand with a very strong foundation. So you can sparkle that value of yours.

**'Whether you think you can or you think you can't, you're right.'**

*Henry Ford*

# Part 1

# What is a brand? What is branding?

**1a**

# What is a brand?

(And why do you need one?)

## A brand is a means of identifying your goods and services in the marketplace… …so basically, a brand is *a badge*

The primary role of any brand is to identify, signify, and distinguish its offering. Why do you need a brand? To stand out from your competitors and be recognisable.

A “brand” is the identifying sign that fans come to trust, wherever they are in the world. So, ultimately, a brand is a badge. A badge of origin.

Of course, a brand is much much more than just a badge—it is a world, and must bear every last level of scrutiny from the cursory glance it gets from a pasty-eating passer-by to the in-depth analysis it might receive from a potential buyer—but seeing your brand firstly as your ‘badge’ helps to begin any journey of brand creation and discovery.

When someone finds something that works for them: a neural connection is made between them and the thing. It is both physical and psychological.

There was once a Russian physiologist called Ivan who did tests on some dogs. He noticed that if you ring a bell every time you feed a dog, the dog associates the food with the bell and the bell with the food. When Ivan rang bells at the start of the experiment, the dogs just looked at him and shrugged. But after many weeks of psychological conditioning and association, every time he rang the bell, the dogs would start salivating

By using physical means, Ivan Pavlov created a psychological equation in the dog’s head, and greatly advanced humanity’s understanding of conditioning.

Bell = food.

And it’s the same with branding.

X = Y.

A brand is a badge of identity that people can use to identify that which they desire and require in the future, ‘whenever I see that brand X I know I will get Y.’

A brand is a badge. A stamp, a mark, a seal of quality, an anchor, an assurance, a promise, a connection, a friend. The trusted friend your audience looks for amid the complexity, pain, and recurring bathos of existence, while they binge carbs, and agree to accept cookies.

Once the emotional connection between the audience and Brand X exists, once everyone knows what badge or symbols to look out for—a logo, a product, brand colours, store location, people, uniform, etc—then it's just a simple matter of maintaining those connections through considered consistency.

Considered consistency. You can have that.

Always considerately reminding people that here is something that they can refer to and return to. A friendly badge that the brand's end-user knows will flick their switch. If you put good food in front of a person, they will start drooling, but they'll also start looking around for mental clues on how to secure the food again in the future. Associations get made in the mind.

If your customer associates your brand identity with your food they will think about your tasty burritos every time they see your logo. They could be miles away but they spy that cheeky Chicken winking at them and it's drooling all round. And it doesn't stop with logos. If done well, your identity can be communicated through all manner of sense data: materials, colours, people, shapes, sounds, and even music. McDonald's has distilled its entire value offering into five notes. G - F - E - C - G. I'm lovin' that. See what I did there?

## ...a brand is also a *means of selling ideas* (so humans can adopt them)

A brand can be anything really.

Within reason. A product, a person, a system, a service, or any combination of such. It can be a commanding fleet of cruise liners, a pump manufacturer, an airline, a dog-friendly campsite, a publisher of Islamic books, a producer of Christmas decorations, a tailor of Jewish headwear, a tuner of Shinto instruments, a Buddhist retreat, a successful chain of spray tan specialists, a range of silicone-based lubricants, a late-night donut parlour, a pick-your-own pumpkin farm or a molecular compound first found in a rare Venezuelan peanut that is now synthesised, reproduced in abundance and readily distributed in little foil blister packs as a trusted hemorrhoid remedy. The important thing to remember is that a brand is foremost a gestalt.

A what?'

A gestalt, or rather—for people who speak plain English—a brand, is just an idea.

Brands are just ideas.

'Ideas...' you scoff, towelling your underparts, 'are abstract, invisible, and difficult to communicate. They are open to misinterpretation. They get garbled and do not travel well!'

My point exactly. But you see, here's the thing: a brand is no ordinary idea. A brand is a special idea: a paratrooper of an idea that is able to be made manifest, communicated and interpreted positively: to leverage and add value to the sum of its parts.

An idea that can be understood.

And embraced.

And shared by flute-blowing pixies and [other].

An idea that people can fall in love with.

Like grass skiing, package holidays, or a political movement.

Now, I should say that the three examples above are generic terms but a brand is a special kind of idea that can be copyrighted and protected. And so a brand is an idea that needs to be unique, distinctive, and original. And so a brand will always need to be a proper noun.

Like Velcro®.

But the bigger point here is that whether a brand's primary identity is a national flag that transcends language or a funky logo with a stylish font, the underlying principle is the same: a brand is an idea that needs to achieve and retain "audience buy-in".

## ...a brand is also a sail, a lever, a pizza *and* a party

Before the advent of the engine, if you wanted to take a boat across a lake you had two choices: arm power or wind. Some may have harnessed dolphins but they would have been in the minority.

But my point is this, on windy days you raised your sail and let the wind take you. And on less windy days, you affixed your oar so it could pivot around a fixed point and when you applied force to one end, the power to the paddle at its business end was amplified. An oar is a lever and the motion of using an oar is called leverage.

Yes, yes, I'm getting to it.

A brand is like a sail and a lever. It is a tool that harnesses the power of external forces and lets you apply "leverage" to amplify your work and make optimal use of your environment. So you can fare well.

The term 'leverage' has a few meanings, sure.

But all of these revolve around the same core concept: using things to amplify things.

In business parlance 'leverage' is most often used to describe the practice of actually borrowing money to generate even greater growth and return on investment—but the term can be used in a more general way to describe the act of using things to create and amplify emergent value for example using a lever to prise open a treasure chest.

A brand is a tool that enables you to create emergent value i.e. value greater than the sum of its parts.

It's like a pizza. Which really, when stripped down to its core components, is just bread, tomato, and cheese. That's it, that's the fundamentals. Pane, pomodoro, formaggi.

Only it's so much more.

Because the cook took the bread, the tomato, and the cheese, and rather than just selling them individually as separate commodities, invested time, love, and creativity and made something new from the constituent parts.

A pizza is more than the sum of its parts.

It's like a party. All the things that make up a party—drinks, pork pies, Malcolm and Sue from next door—are really quite dull on their own, but put us all in a room together and: boom, we're now doing a conga to Feeling Hot.

'Steady, Malcolm! You'll put your back out!'

Airbnb is a great example of leverage. In 2022 it had revenue of 8.4 billion USD and did so without physically owning a single room. Now, obviously, the actual Ability, and the rather clever business idea, of Airbnb (how its platform and operational systems continue to enable 300 million end-users in thousands of towns and cities across the world to easily find and provide accommodation) is a key reason behind its success, however, it is the brand name and identity that makes all this possible. It is a vital part of Airbnb's success as a digital "gateway" or "fixer" for its end-users.

No one ever got rich without leverage. Life needs leverage—of some kind—to improve its standing and circumstances. Life itself is only possible through the wise and beautiful leverage of available resources over time.

Life levered itself out of the primordial clay. The employment of leverage—whether that's photosynthesis, mitochondria, opposable thumbs, adaptability, natural selection, use of stone tools, use of wheels, use of fire, use of pizza ovens—has enabled life to express itself in myriad ways. Had it not bothered, we would not be here.

The employment of leverage has enabled groups of people to form tribes—corporations, religions, nations, and international organisations—and create things greater than the sum of their parts.

A business may be able to do many things, but most often it is the brand that makes everything possible.

Most often the brand is the fixed point or gravitational centre that holds everything in place. The point around which you apply a force that is then magnified. That isn't because of any one particular element like the brand's offering, or its name, strapline or logo, or Swiss typeface, but because together all these parts, based on an initial guided intention—a good why and a good ethos—create a central force that gives everything meaning, momentum, and order, and emergent value. The centre that holds the magic together: the people, the processes, the cash flow, the capital. The brand is the mother that every successful well-balanced commercial endeavour needs to grow and release its latent energy. A brand is the camp fire that attracts, holds and energises the group.

'Brand Power!'—as I like to shout in the faces of unsuspecting pedestrians —'is all about leveraging resources to maximise return on investment'.

## ...a brand is *a stage*

A brand—like life—is a stage, and you, as brand creator, or "Brand Angel", are the Stage Director. It is your job to create great performances. For millennia, the "stage" has been the place audiences have looked to for excitement, for answers, for consolation—it is the area of promise that waits under the spotlight saying 'Here you may witness an expression we hope you will find meaningful.'

This book is a stage for my thoughts, expressed as words.

Stages are important to humans, we respect them as vital bridging points between minds, between imagination and reality. Stages are opportunities to frame information, disclose meaningful sequences, broadcast, connect with people, and affirm things, and question things, together. To help us develop our relationships. And nothing is more powerful, or meaningful, to humans than relationships.

Stages have the power to educate, inspire, and heal. And provide us with opportunities to connect with others and console and inspire ourselves. They allow us to explore every aspect of existence, the plentiful gamut of humanity, from apples to oranges, ethics to economics, religion to anal bleaching. Who's to say which data is more worthy of appreciation? When scientists and experts are divided on which questions to ask and which answers to seek, a brand can be the most important stage its audience looks at. Do not waste the opportunity to speak your truth.

Branding is framing, but it is also about setting the scene to "lever" a greater sense of occasion. Stages create spectacle. Is there anything greater than the FIFA World Cup? An event so joyous in its sense of "carnival"—its sense of bringing the world together through football—it makes everything become resplendent with international glamour. The sport becomes important to those otherwise uninterested in football, the host nation becomes exciting and even the dry-humoured punditry about disputed free kicks becomes something of great beauty. Everyone plays their part and performs upon this great world stage.

Stages and platforms elevate that which they present to the world.

If you take a world-class violinist and put her in The Royal Albert Hall, she will be thrown roses, if you put her in the tube station five minutes down the road, she'll be thrown pennies. *If* she's lucky.

In Part Six I will introduce you to the A.C.T. Philosophy and show how a brand can best express itself through its Abilities, Content, and Touchpoints.

I will also show how the *Theatre!* of branding is deeply important in the art of selling, and how one should be keenly aware of the value of performance. We live in an "experience economy"* and delivering experiential *Theatre!* is an effective means of attracting, retaining, and touching your audience.

* I recommend the book *The Experience Economy*, by B. Joseph Pine II and James H. Gilmore.

'All the world's a stage
and most of us are
desperately unrehearsed.'
*Sean O'Casey*

## ...a brand is also *a hill of beans*

Long-term success, in any venture, is won—and in fact, can only be won—through building up enough beans to call yourself a hill of beans. But at what point can you call a hill a hill? After two beans? Ten? Two hundred? More?

It's the same with building a brand. At what point can you call a brand 'a brand'? After having the idea? After coming up with a name? After designing its identity? After printing the business cards? After your first customer? After your first hundred successful transactions? Your first million in turnover?

Really, the answer is when you god damn' well say it is ... however, there are many obstacles one must overcome and milestones one must achieve before one really gets the success they desire and deserve.

The trick is to be so good they cannot ignore you. To be undeniable. And the more you wisely invest in your brand—and the more time you put into attaining experience and expertise and rolling with the blows and failures—the more credibility your brand will earn in the marketplace over time.

Whatever metric you use to measure success, there'll always be someone with more than you. More followers, likes and views, but stay cool, and focused, and never be too desperate to show off, lie, or exaggerate your position. It's tempting to burst out the door half-cocked with a handful of beans and say you're the best brand since sliced bread, but if you stake too much on too little you may trip and spill your beans. As the US military says, 'Two is one and one is none'. They are talking about reserves and redundancies (backup systems) and how no plan survives first contact with the enemy.

Humans remain successful as a species, in that we exist, and a great reason for that continued existence is because baked within our DNA lies a lot of redundancy. Thanks to our well-evolved genes we can adapt to a variety of situations, and furthermore, we carry dormant genes that wait for opportunities to display even greater latitude.

Never be too bitter or angry with slip-ups, or set-backs, or slow rates of progress because ultimately these obstacles, if handled correctly, can imbue one with greater operational proficiency, a richer, more well-rounded world-view, and of course wisdom, and better anecdotes.

Great brands take time to build, slowly slowly, one bean after the next, year after year, after year, until one day, you become an overnight success.

Building up experience, fans, and trust through Abilities, Content, and Touchpoints takes time, creativity, nerve, sweat, and patience. But you must keep at it.

Success in life does not come from one idea or one thought. Life is not about having that one perfect scheme and then relaxing with your feet up. Success comes from habit and commitment. Life is about constantly wriggling out of the straitjacket.

We conquer by continuing.

---

'After climbing a great hill,
one finds that there are many
more hills to climb.'
*Nelson Mandela*

---

## ***Why*** **give yourself a brand?**

To create something tangible, and meaningful, that you can show others and say 'I made this'. To give your value offerings more leverage. To attract an audience of fans and team members. To retain that audience. To scale your value. To build up brand equity to atomise your offerings, or one day sell your business/brand (or franchise it, or license it). To partner up or enter into co-branding initiatives. To achieve Peak Fun. To live your best life. To help others and make the world a better place.

'But I am an artist!' you scream, 'I can't scale up, it's just me! No one can do what I do!'

Sure, the lone individual cannot be duplicated ... but the personal brand of an individual enables them to scale many things, and amplify value. As a personal brand, you can "productise" your expertise, goods, and services. If you're a famous boxer, a strong brand helps you put your name on saleable things (yes, I'm looking at you George Foreman). If you're not a famous boxer, don't panic. You just need to be known about by your audience. If your audience sees you and sees you could be of value, and sees you are trustworthy, then it's game on, you have a brand that can be scaled.

You might be accustomed to selling your time for money but with a strong personal brand, you can create massive value. You can scale up. You can create eLearning programs, books, videos, and all manner of exotic paraphernalia and generate passive income streams to complement or supersede the personal services you provide. So chill out and read on.

---

'A brand is simply trust.'
*Steve Jobs*

---

## **...and a brand comes from *the process of branding.***

**1b**

# What is branding?

(And do you really need to do it?)

## Branding is how you differentiate yourself

If I had to explain branding in one short line I would say 'branding is how you differentiate yourself'. By that I mean, branding is the means you use to differentiate your offering to people, for example how you choose to dress your trade.

'Why?' asks Uncle Brian. 'Why differentiate yourself?'

Good question, Brian.*

Differentiating your brand—and your goods or services—from other brands:

– ensures you create a meaningful connection between your brand and an audience of loyal fans, so you get future business

– ensures *your* loyal fans do not use another similar brand, by mistake, instead of your brand

– ensures the loyal fans of *another brand* do not use your brand, by mistake.

> Obviously, you *can* steal the loyal fans of another brand†, however, you should do it by attracting them to your own distinct offering. I. e. they should come to you because they want to check you out on your own merits, through curiosity, and not by mistake or deception.

It's important you differentiate your brand from other brands so you stand out and be counted for either the original things you create and bring to the world, or the unique way you serve people and do business, so you create your own authentic audience of end-users. People who dig you.

And of course, it's important to differentiate your brand from others for legal reasons.

If you appear too similar to another brand—whether by intention or mistake—and if the other brand can prove it existed before you and can show where you are too similar—painful and expensive lawsuits can be brought against you, which may result in you having to change your brand or remove it from the marketplace. Whether by intention or accident, it's still painful.

If you *are too similar to another brand by mistake*—if you create your brand and its means of dress and service offering, in good conscience, believing you were being unique and original—you can still be accused

* Uncle Brian is my imaginary friend.

† Provided it is lawful and doesn't breach any contracts you've signed.

of failing to do enough due diligence or research about the marketplace, especially so if the similarity occurs in the same industry sector or field.

If you *are too similar to another brand by intention*—if your brand is attempting to harness another brand's hard-earned reputation, goodwill, protected IP (Intellectual Property), or patented idea—you can be accused of 'passing off' or copyright infringement.

If you *appear almost identical to another brand*—and it is made evident you are actively seeking to sell replicas or counterfeit goods—you will most probably face public prosecution (see Trademark Counterfeiting Act of 1984).

In short, it's important to differentiate your brand, that is to say, to make it different from others, so as not to be mistaken for another.

A brand achieves differentiation through its Abilities, Content, and Touchpoints, using its unique name, line, identity, style, and voice.

(Your brand's why and ethos are also vital considerations when you differentiate yourself—and are precious parts of your brand's foundation—however, they are "invisible" aspects of your brand's presentation to the world, and effectively irrelevant "above the surface" in the tangible trade-based marketplace of sensual connection.)

## ...branding is *the way you tell people what you do* (and what you can offer)

If the first rule of branding is 'show people how you're different', then the second rule is simply 'tell people what you do'.

On the "Playing Field of Life", fortune depends largely on what one is able to do, and in harnessing one's abilities, one is able to better oneself but only when those abilities give value to someone else—only when your offering is known about, wanted, and valued. This is all down to a little something I like to call the "universal law of exchange".

When social, conscious beings live together, they play on each individual's particular strengths to optimise the group, be that family, village, or world. One person might make good strawberry jam but is allergic to paint, and another person loves painting but cannot cook. 'I'll paint your house, you make me some jam and we'll invent some kind of money system to transfer the respective values because I love your jam—but you can't pay me completely in jam.'

When we lived together in small bands of roaming hominids, setting up camp in makeshift hamlets, and villages, we all knew what everyone did. And we knew who made the jam...

'Alfred makes the jam!'

..but now, we all live in a *global* village—so we don't know who's doing what. There are upsides and downsides to living in a bigger populace. The opportunities to scale and make meaningful transfers are amplified but so is the problem of getting known, gaining trust, and outshining the competition.

Whether your offering is local or international, whether it's sales training, the importation of olive oil, personal fitness, or white water rafting, branding is a profoundly effective tool and process that helps you communicate that offering to people.

> Marketing, PR, and sales are also practices that communicate your offering to your audience, however, these are usually more proactive and direct means of communication. Whereas branding is a subtle, intelligent, and patient form of communication. Branding enables you to "dress" and "position" your offering at the source, so it can optimise your offering in the marketplace.

Branding has a very organic relationship with marketing, PR, and sales—and we will look at these more direct forms of demand generation and customer conversion later in the A.C.T. section—but for now, in the interests of meaningful learning, this book is going to first concentrate on the foundational aspects of the brand building process.

Essentially, at this point, we are simply outlining that branding is about packaging all your skills and offerings into one "bucket" that distinguishes you from your competitors.

---

'We need to define what it is about you or your group
that will form the foundation of your brand.'
*Luke Arwen Shaw*

---

## ...branding *creates better agreement* (between buyer and seller)

When you brand a thing—or things—you put it in a box and tag it. The seller does this physically with care and thought, with packaging, positioning, and a price tag, and the buyer does this mentally with a perceptual tag.

'I think that's worth about fifty quid.'

If the value of both tags lines up, kerching!, you both agree on the value and it's business time. And if the price is cheaper than the buyer's perception, they can't get their wallet out fast enough ... 'Yes, yes, I do believe in the beauty of this silver case and the value of this workmanship, and it certainly is worth £43.99.'

Overpricing can be a way of losing custom but equally beware of underpricing. If the seller's tag is too low, alarm bells will go off, 'what's wrong with it?' thinks the buyer.

Imagine I show you two similar products with Product A priced at £200 and Product B priced at £500. Which one do you perceive to be better? It's B, isn't it?

Branding is a means of presenting a seller's offering in such a way that the "Story of Value" gets conveyed to the buyer.

Branding allows you to position your offerings to optimise their perceived value and to ensure your proposition agrees with your end-user's perception.

## ...branding is also *a subtle and sophisticated form of communication*, based on managed presumption within a tribal system

Branding presumes the audience will "get it".

There is educated presumption and there is not-so-educated presumption but all branding—like all communication—relies on presumption.

And because presumption creates efficiency, we humans employ it.

No matter your position in your "tribe", the overall efficiency of everything is important. Whether you're an employer or an employee, you need to take advantage of the tribal "systems of governance" so you can survive and better yourself, either to generate better conditions for your loved dependents or to enhance your status and "currency" within the tribe.

Humans are social, conscious, status-oriented, incentive-driven beings who love nothing more than self-betterment within a group. And if you don't take advantage of efficiency and leverage, you fall behind. You get laughed at by the others.

'Look at Lionel still doing that!'

Efficiencies are respected all around town.

It is for this reason, communication is based on presumption.

When someone says 'This car is eco-friendly' they of course believe that those to whom they direct their communication know what a 'car' is and what 'eco-friendly' means. They assume the audience can speak English. They are also assuming the audience cares and values the term 'eco-friendly'.

Each human has its own tribes—you'll know which yours are—and each tribe has its own brands. The tribal values, as you perceive them, significantly influence your actions. 'People like us, do things like this.'

Tribes vary in their proclivities but many share the same basic shape, often coloured by the wider social, cultural, and environmental conditions in which the tribes coexist. Many tribes share the belief that it's more socially acceptable to take the family to a coffee shop on a Saturday than to, say, a strip club. Tribal values—as you perceive and interpret them—influence your decisions and actions.

I expect you live in the modern world, belong to more than one tribe, and that you recognise that different tribes value different brands. A teenager's new trainers usually have more currency in his social tribe than in his family tribe because his status at home is not influenced by his footwear.

---

'A tribe is a group of people connected to one another, connected to a leader, and connected to an idea. For millions of years, human beings have been part of one tribe or another. A group needs only two things to be a tribe: a shared interest and a way to communicate.'
*Seth Godin, Tribes: We Need You to Lead Us*

---

## ...branding is also *focused choice*

At every level, at every stage, when creating your brand, there are choices along the way.

Do we use red, blue, pink, orange? If red, what type of red? Warm red or sexy red? Is that red too angry? Should we use cotton, leather, or maybe pleather?

SHOULD WE SHOUT, or should we whisper?

Choices make you who you are. A brand is just a series of choices. And focus is key. Branding is simply choosing which things we want to pursue and which qualities we want to amplify and celebrate.

Good branding is not about lying, it's about selective expression. It's about what you choose to express and what you choose to not express. And that choice and focus gives us direction, which manages expectation.

Focus on the things that matter.

James Brown couldn't play an instrument that well. Queen Elizabeth II was not so great at Formula One—but did they spend their time focusing on those shortcomings? We think of JB as the 'Godfather of Soul' not a failure in music. And the beloved late queen is not seen as a lesser to Lewis Hamilton.

Branding is about crystallising your key offering into a simple and coherent yet infinitely engaging series of Touchpoints and expressions with consistency. A brand is the sum of all its choices. We are what we do, but we are also what we do not do. And so the chapters of this book are designed to lead you through the branding process in a step-by-step way, ensuring you focus on and choose the right things at the right time.

When you decorate a house, you follow certain steps. So it is with building the foundation for your brand, you wouldn't decorate your store, give out your business cards, or host an event before coming up with your brand name.

---

'Your life is a result of the choices you have made. If you don't like your life, start making better choices.'
*Zig Ziglar*

---

## ...branding is *a reminder*

Your short-term memory does exactly what it says on the tin, it holds your memories for a 'short term'.

In my case, it's a *very* short term.

There is a set limit of information it can hold. Unless the experience was truly memorable—or I made a special effort to remember it using memory hacks—my brain will bin the memory the first chance it gets. I suspect this is just to make room for new memories, which it will also dump, and continue to dump, ad infinitum.

That's why the brand that creates and delivers distinctive and memorable Touchpoints—with frequency—will become a brand that is recalled, talked about, and used.

Branding is a constant reminder, to both ourselves and our audiences, of what we're good at and why we're here.

We forget our inspirations, we lose faith in our convictions and our memories are traitors to our long-term needs but having a strong brand behind you is a serious advantage. All that levered power working in your favour, in your interests. All that copyrighted and fully endorsed content to refer to. A mesmerising and fully-branded network of Touchpoints, an impressive constellation of partners and suppliers. A history of success, all wrapped up with a heartening back story and beautifully understated logo. All someone need do is drop your brand name into a Google window and kerpow!, what do they see? What powerful evidence is presented to them of the value your brand provides and the impact it makes?

## ...branding *touches people* (over time)

The first rule of branding: no one cares about your brand. Really, they don't.

Until of course, they do.

And then the level to which they care will lie in direct proportion to how much your brand touches them. To its audience of end-users, a brand is simply a series of touchpoints over time.

But for the purposes of this training program, we are calling them Touchpoints (with a big T).

As I said at the start, and repeat now (because repetition is the mother of learning), Touchpoints are the places where your brand and your audience touch each other ... and each Touchpoint is an opportunity to make or break a valuable connection.

A brand's product is a Touchpoint.

A donut is a Touchpoint.

We touch things all day long. I am currently touching an Apple product.

And in branding, you must consider where best, how best, and when best, to touch your audiences.

If you're an airline you touch your end-user dozens of times in any single journey, from the ticket purchase to the boarding experience, to the quality of seating, snacks, toilets, and general travel enjoyment.

And any one of those is an opportunity to please or annoy people. And most, if not all people, are humans ... and humans are hard-wired to overlook things going well (good design is invisible) and notice only the things that go wrong.

When many think of branding they think of logos, above-the-line advert campaigns, and jingles. And while these remain vital ways of establishing brand presence, they are really just the tip of the iceberg in terms of winning hearts and minds. Below the surface, beneath the brochures, logos, and advertorials,* below the surface circus of Likes and testimonials, stir unspoken emotions in private hearts. Private hearts that are ultimately responsible for clicks and footfall. Good branding is much more than fonts, colours, and billboards, it is every single place your brand touches—and transforms—its end-user.

## ...branding is also *considered* consistency

'Can I trust you?'

This question is everything to a human.

It is really all we need to know about something or someone.

'Are you going to hurt me or rip me off or make me look stupid?'

'Well? Are you?'

In business—as in life—trust is valuable, but it's not so easy to acquire.

* An 'advertorial' is a paid for advert in the style of an editorial or objective journalistic article.

Branding can encourage trust but one must put in the time and not expect immediate results.

Patience, young grasshopper.

Reputations take years to develop and seconds to destroy. Trust is a valuable, vulnerable thing and it only grows when the conditions are right. And when cared for over a certain period.

'Yeah, yeah,' snarls Gaz,* eyeballing end-of-quarter targets. 'Whatev's.'

Patience, Gaz, it's true. Humans have psychological features in place that act like warning systems. To guard against getting hurt, again, we file bad experiences using whatever information it can to identify you and anything *like* you. And given that the human brain must filter through thousands of bits of information every day, it demonstrates an incredible ability to ignore swathes of data that it deems relevant while avoiding that which it deems dangerous.

Because branding is such a powerful lever, it is vital to be aware of how much it can amplify people's ability to love, hate, or ignore you. And so good branding is about scaling trust. And trust is achieved through the consistency and authenticity of your integrity.

So, the simple answer is this: do the right thing, all the time.

Consistency of behaviour, and messaging, help build trust in the marketplace and fortify your brand's integrity. This means people will like your brand more and will be more likely to engage with it.

The merchant who shows up and honours her promise with consistent behaviour and messaging and proven success, time after time, earns integrity and trust and a special place in peoples' hearts.

To do this you need to have both authority and flavour; you need to stay "edible and credible" in ways that "tease and please". And you often need to do this while enduring the initial phase of—and perhaps many other times of—low trade.

Branding can accelerate the build of a trusted reputation and provide you with some cover during downturns. And of course, even the biggest and most successful brands can hit slumps in trading activity.

Like many businesses, Airbnb experienced great challenges during the COVID-19 pandemic—and in 2020 reported losses of billions of dollars—but because it had such a strong platform, and reputable brand in place, it was able to bounce back to full health.

* Gaz is another of my imaginary friends. A reckless carb-chomping executive. Driven yet blinkered.

No matter the pain, excuse, or hardship, you must "show up" for your end-users. Connect and repeat. Connect and repeat. Connect and repeat.

And always with fresh thinking and presence of mind.

Never take your audience for granted.

Familiarity builds trust but it also breeds contempt. So you need to be reliable but also compelling: "a brick with a tick".

Good branding is consistent and considered expression.

Not easy.

To overcome this monumental challenge you need to "use every part of the cow" and leverage as much value from your environment and your resources as possible.

Chief among those resources is your brand.

Use your brand to build your brand. And be consistent.

Consistency counts.

Not necessarily consistency in offering—as we have seen with such brands as Amazon and Virgin, who have been able to scale trust and brand equity and venture into new areas—but certainly consistency of name, line, identity, style, and voice. And how you touch and transform your audience via your ACTivity which is guided by your why and ethos.

Branding is consistency of landscape over any particular customer journey.

This is especially important in non-human processes or automated events like online purchases. If someone sees something they like on your website and tries to buy it, there must be a guided journey or process that constantly assures the customer that they are still safely inside your process. If they are bounced over to a third party it must be well-signposted otherwise it could feel like a mistake, a trick, or a disconnect. And the customer may bolt like a deer in the woods.

If I buy something from a brand online, I want to feel I'm being handled by that same brand every step of the way, including the checkout page, *and* I will want to receive a receipt email featuring the same brand identity, style, and voice that I began the process with.

A story.

One event with a beginning, a middle, and an end.

Trust is earned through consistent practical acts.

The more consistent the experience, the happier customers are. Also, the experience will smooth the way for future purchases.

Branding is saying 'This is who we are, and this is why we matter', over and over again. It's expression through sustained yet infinitely engaging repetition.

Stay fresh and add surprise but don't change the formula your audience clearly likes. Don't fix what ain't broke. Look at the popular noodle restaurant brand Wagamama. It manages to deliver a distinctive offering and process from location to location, the same each time. You know that the Teppanyaki, Ramen, Donburi, and Itame Yasai will taste the same—whether you're in Guildford, Coventry, or Boston, USA. It is the same model McDonald's launched back in the 1950s. Uniform uniqueness. Considered consistency.

## ...branding *creates a world* (of intellectual property, that you own)

People need places to go. Private spaces to recharge in, or public spaces to commune in. When you give yourself a brand, you create a world, distinct from anything that has come before. A world others can visit to find health, happiness, answers, joy, relationships, solace, and consolation. Things they cannot find out there, in the real world amid the "Dance of Conformity" our professional and social obligations bid us to participate in.

Branding is an art. The art of choosing which parts of the data to focus on, so you can position yourself as an authentic world-builder and create a space your audience will be attracted to and enjoy spending time in, through connection with your offerings.

If you know the character and terrain of your world you can focus on the right things.

To keep it all "on brand".

Most sports brands don't focus too much on creating deep-fried food, and most fast food brands don't focus too much on deep space tourism.

People want different things from life—some want to be cosseted inside away from the germs and pollution, saluted and waited on hand and foot, others want to be out where the music's playing—but if you can give people what they want through your brand, you give them a world. You create a credible place your fans can inhabit and if you create unique Touchpoints and Content, this world becomes a world of your Intellectual Property (IP).

A brand is a clearly definable world that you, and those you attract, build, to make the real world richer in the process. Branding is a wonderful means of creative expression that can have its own language, culture, and spaces.

Whether your brand is about sport, handbags, music, theatre, medical supplies, or wholefoods, you can create it, own it and control it. And because you own it and control it, you can sell it. And because you own it and control it, where do you think the money earned from sales goes?

That's right, the rights owner, and that is you, because you own that which was sold (minus the tax, of course).

Welcome to Business Success 101.

If you sell Mickey Mouse-branded watches you will need a special licence because your brand is not Walt Disney. However, if what you sell is not beholden to any other rights-owner, if what you sell has been given special value by virtue of the work your inimitable brand does, if for example the wooden tables, coffee beans, and labour you buy, comes together to create a popular and distinctive coffee shop brand, then you create a world and your brand becomes your very own DisneyLand.

## ...branding *brings things together*

Branding allows disparate—often opposing—themes, to meet, overlap and make babies. X can play with a Y, commerce can meet art, oil can mix with water.

Branding can provide a wonderful framework conducive to originality and creation where the usual laws and limitations take a holiday and new combinations and paradigms can spark into life. We humans are incentive-driven love machines, but we are also decision engines and we respect and adhere to set boundaries that often seem to hold potential ideas apart. We are "dividers" by nature and nurture. 'You can't mix this with that!'

Branding is an art that asks 'Why not?'

## ...branding is also *sensual*

Branding works by using Touchpoints—places where it touches its audience.

And every place is both a physical place and a mental place.

We humans are conscious beings, not floating clouds of plasma. We experience the bare naked physical world through our senses. Senses that serve up data to our consciousness through our skin, nerves, eyes, and ears—through differences in light and shade, vibration, sound, texture, weight, consistency, odour, temperature, chemistry, and hormonal production. These physical "impressions" act as food for our senses, nervous systems, and minds. From this data we can create, trigger, and influence conscious experience, further changes in body chemistry, further hormonal production, emotions, moods, and memories.

We spend most of our waking life immersed in some form of sensual event. We feel air pressure, humidity, the wonderful sound of Velcro®, and the taste of tomato sauce. We devour pizza, we process nutrients, we wee, expel, and wash our hands. We touch that which we like to touch, or need to touch, smell that which we like to smell or have to smell. We surround ourselves with tangible things that make us feel a certain way. We are attracted to—and wish to hold onto—that which pleases our senses and we are *repelled from* anything that flushes us with discomfort. We humans foremost experience life through the mind which uses senses, to make sense of—and apply meaning to—everything.

Good branding takes this into consideration.

## ...branding is also *positioning*

We live in a world of perception and a lot of branding is simply positioning. Positioning influences perception.

A few years ago I was working as a freelance graphic designer, bouncing from one placement to the next. On one particular job—due to 'desk shortages'—I was assigned a small makeshift desk by the printer. I found it hard to concentrate with people standing over my shoulder all day long, waiting for printouts. Apart from a few who assumed I was a repairman—and asked me how to use the printer—most left me alone as if I were invisible. In fact, one guy, deep in conversation on his phone, actually tried to sit on me, before acknowledging his mistake with a firm manly pat on my shoulder. All the distractions and explanations delayed my working speed and the person I was reporting to seemed deeply unimpressed with my output. However, to my surprise, I was invited back a few months later, and sure enough there were still desk shortages. But this time, someone else was using my printer desk, so I was asked to use the boss's glass-walled corner office. I set to work but soon became aware of people walking past and whispering to one another about who I could possibly be. Obviously someone of great importance, perhaps a personal friend of the boss, perhaps someone brought in to make redundancies. Honestly, this did happen. I know a group of impressed young executives when I see one.

This trait of discriminatory judgment—and positioning accordingly—is, ironically, something we pretty much all have in common.

We process things based on assumptions, assumptions based on associations. We are status-oriented for the most part and we tug our forelocks when we see a famous person (yes, I know cynical Uncle Brian will dispute this but he would lose his mind if he saw Kate Bush in Sainsbury's).

Power is an aphrodisiac. We jump to conclusions. We're lazy, pretentious, and impatient. We haven't got time to question everything the world presents us with. And presumption allows greater efficiency.

Yes, the greater part of a person's true power and value lies in what is not seen ... but humans are visual creatures who prejudge to save time and we each create "rulebooks" of what things mean, and we build our lives around those accordingly.

<u>It pays to be aware of what your presentation and position say about you and your offering.</u>

It's quicker.

Even if you wish to subvert or ignore those rulebooks, it's valuable to know first, what people perceive.

Cubist painters learned first how to paint traditionally before they bent the rules. New comedians want to bring new things into the world and often ridicule the cheesy dad jokes of yesteryear, but they first have to know what those jokes were, otherwise, they may inadvertently repeat them, and find out that so-and-so did that joke in 1952, which is a humbling discovery.

Try to be aware of what your audience knows and what they are perceiving. Listen to people. Observe. Ask questions. Use online questionnaires, and “unpack” the picture.

Feedback is fundamental.

Study the history of the tribe, and position your brand to serve its aims. The wise see the beauty hidden from a fool, but most fools see that which they are presented with.

Don’t be a fool. Think. Be reflective.

Don’t present a completely false picture—because people are often in fact more intelligent than you give them credit for and you’ll probably be found out and discredited—but equally, there is probably more leeway in your own presentational prowess than you can imagine.

To see what your audience is seeing, you must observe and take the time to reflect honestly. You need to know the world, and you need to know yourself.

The more reflective you are, the easier it is to be true to thine own self.

So give yourself a long, hard look in the mirror...

# Part 2

# Give yourself a long, hard look in the mirror

Building a brand is tricky.

The stakes can be high, the odds of success low, and the variables hard to keep track of. People are unpredictable. The future is unknown. But one thing is sure, every website you visit demands first your stance on cookies.

'Well?' it demands, 'Do you accept them?'

It can be tedious.

But nothing good was ever easy. So here are a few general thoughts to put some peace in your mind and fire in your belly. After all, the best way to predict the future is to create it.

## Boss the butterflies

Building your own brand requires change. And I'm not talking about loose coinage here, I'm talking about deviation. And not latex bodysuit deviation but deviating from your normal path and venturing into parts unknown. And that's scary. So, it's a good idea to prepare for it.

Fear, that is. In small, practical ways where possible.

One first step would be to add preparation to our small list of things to give oneself at this early stage.

Motivation. Approval. Patience. And **Preparation.**

It's messed up my MAP acronym but hey ho, MAPP is fine, this needs to be said. General fear is coming, and with it a whole range of pressures so it's important you prepare.

But don't *over*-prepare. God, no. Perfectionism can kill many a dream. We all know that that which comes fast and easy is usually inferior to that which comes slow and hard (yes, I'm looking at you Heinz tomato ketchup), however, there are some times where you need to pump the gas and throw hesitancy to the wind like a well-padded stuntman.

And that's the image I want us to move forward with, a well-padded stuntman. Dynamic, eager, and ready for action, but prepared in various places by protective padding.

Pretty soon, if we're serious about this new brand thing, we are going to have to leap into the unknown and embrace the painful notion of change. And because you are a real and well-balanced human—and not some pathological robot*—that is scary.

Fear has authority. But it *can* be managed.

As I always say, nerves are natural, and butterflies are ok, but if they're flying in formation what could go wrong?

(Hard cut to me in traction.)

---

'It takes courage to grow up and become who you really are.'
*E. E. Cummings*

---

* No offence meant if you are actually a pathological robot.

Now, I'm no Wim Hof, and I'm sure there are better experts in the field of endurance and stress management than myself (such as David Goggins, Jocko Willink, Amelia Boone, Mel Robbins, Jen Sincero et al) ... but I have endured long periods of uncertainty when setting up new ventures so, I can offer *some* advice.

Everyone's different, and people will find different things to help them negotiate the tricky path, but I know what has worked for me.

Chocolate milk and Dark Wave music.

I guarantee they *might* help you become a better person.

If used in moderation, where appropriate.

If you need other ideas (beyond diet, hydration and music) I might also suggest sleep, attitude, running, and modern dance, but I guess we all need to find what works for us.

Do take time to find things that work for you. Do take time to put padding in place. And definitely do consider mind tricks.

Seek out proven techniques that can enhance your psychological wellbeing, mental clarity, and neural firepower.*

It's hard to be lucid and dynamic when you're scared, frazzled, or depressed, so by experimenting new ways of reconsidering the world, much like a shopper trying on jackets, you're likely to find a lifehack that works. In preparation for challenges ahead.

One trick that works for me is that of reframing problems.

The recognition of a new problem usually triggers in me instant bad feelings, which, in turn, set off a series of biochemical domino rallies, each one a cascading firestorm of synaptic pathways that were probably laid down during difficult unresolved parts of my formative years when I was bullied for wearing a bowl-cut hairstyle. And so, very often, I can be feeling great and living my best life, rollerskating through town giving double gun gestures of hello to all and sundry, when I hear something negative like 'look at that moron on rollerskates'. Before I know what time it is the world has become a cruel circus of heartbreak and shame and for a long time this negative response of mine was a big problem.

But then I heard Marcus Aurelis say:

'Choose not to be harmed, and you won't feel harmed. Don't feel harmed—and you haven't been.'

Marcus has been dead for hundreds of years, so I must have read the line, but still, his advice remains useful. Reframing really helps.

* Two books whose practical advice continues to help me better navigate my personal mental wellbeing through the world are: 'Why Has Nobody Told Me This Before?' by Julie Smith and 'The Subtle Art of Not Giving a F*ck' by Mark Manson.

## See everything as a gift

I approach life with cautious scepticism. It's a conditioned response. Growing up with a bowl-cut hairstyle hammered into me the value of vigilance and understatement. A visit to the local shops was risky enough, so attempting yoga in public would have been simply foolish, but as I grow older I do have more time for New Age beliefs.

The more I look at brands, businesses, and organisations, the more I see that those with widespread success and appeal almost always shine with a sense of great peace. I know this probably sounds a strange thing to say and there could *well* be a dash of naive, magical thinking at play, but I would like to take a moment to champion peace and appreciation as key tools to add to our list.

Motivation. Approval. Patience. Preparation. Peace. Appreciation.

MAPPPA, anyone?

Problems are inevitable but how one reacts to them is always a choice.

---

'An animal, struggling against the noose, tightens it.'
*Seneca*

---

'The green reed which bends in the wind is stronger
than the mighty oak which breaks in a storm.'
*Confucius*

---

To build a brand one needs to do more than learn business practices, and how to create email lists, or add gif files to emails ... one needs to learn how to *learn* and often it is through those who have lived lives in extremis that we learn the most.

When Viktor Frankl was committed to a Nazi concentration camp in 1942, just nine months into a new marriage, he saw hellish scenes and heartbreaking cruelty at every turn, including the death of his father. And the nightmare did not cease for years. In 1944, Viktor and the surviving members of his family were sent on to Auschwitz where his mother and brother were murdered in gas chambers. The unrelenting anguish of these vicious acts would be enough to break the strongest spirit, and Viktor saw how the interminable brutality of life in a concentration camp shattered those around him in various ways. He saw how the pessimistic types gave up early but he also saw the cruel way it affected people with more positive mental attitudes and how most of those fell too, and all the harder when they did, from falling psychologically from greater heights. But Viktor, who had been a young psychiatrist before his incarceration, used tremendous psychological power to outwit this inhumane system.

With incredible presence of mind, he found the strength, inspiration, and hope, to endure and survive. And he did this despite losing his wife, who was killed in another camp. He had every reason and excuse to withdraw from the world, and yet he endured to tell his story and devoted the rest of his life to helping humanity find sense and meaning despite his first-hand knowledge of how low we can fall.

Had he railed against the conditions he experienced he may have lost faith, or he may have been put against a wall and shot. But he hacked the system. The bigger system. Yes, he knew the Nazi system was immoral and inhuman, but by radical acceptance and zen-like consciousness, he was able to absorb and transform the negative energies all around him. He became grateful for the experience. He would thank everything that came to him, blessing the oppressive guards, inedible food, and heart-wrenching testimonies.

If you always choose to see the present moment as a gift, you are more likely to use it to better serve you. It's not what happens, it's how you frame what happens.

---

'Change the way you look at things, and the things you look at change.'
*Max Planck, German physicist*

---

## Who's paying for all this?

Commercial viability is not the only determinant of a brand's worth or success, however, if you want to sustain things over the long-term, you're going to need to cover your running costs. And preferably, turn a profit, where possible.

Living is, and always was, expensive.

The universe is built like that. Eating breakfast expends energy, but the calories the breakfast gives you compensate for this expense, and hopefully leave a calorific profit to get you through to your next meal. The Hunter/Gatherer speculates to accumulate.

If you want to use photography, you need to invest in a camera, a photographer, or a stock library account. If you want a good website, someone needs to put that together. Products? They ain't making themselves. And if you want employees or suppliers, well, you'll need to pay them or they might start moaning. You can of course consider skills-swapping or 'contra-deals' but they are simply other forms of payment or energy transfer. It's that universal law of exchange, again.

Achieving a viable outgo/income cycle is hard work and at the beginning, getting your brand set up and established can be a challenge no matter who you are.

Even big landmark brands were once vulnerable little acorns. Look at FedEx—the courier and delivery brand—its logo is now famous the world over, seen in every office and back street tattoo parlour from Iceland to Mexico. Must have started small and strong, and never faltered right?

Well, not really.

Federal Express, as it was first called, was based on a bold concept entertained by its founder, Fred Smith. The concept of owning every part of a parcel's journey. Fred went for it, poured his own money into the idea and achieved millions in venture capital investment during the company's set-up in the early 1970s. This enabled the company to procure fourteen Dassault Falcon 20 airplanes and connect 25 US cities, which is, let's be fair, a pretty impressive move. However, within two years Federal Express had run into severe financial difficulties and was down to its last $5000, which meant it could no longer afford to cover its running costs and was effectively flat-lining.

So what did Fred do?

He took that $5000 to Las Vegas and threw it onto the Blackjack table. And he won. $27,000.

Just enough cashola to trade for another week and turn the company's fortunes around. And in 2023, according to its annual report, FedEx 'marked 50 years of transforming the world by connecting people and possibilities,' with reported assets worth over $87,000 million.*

Thanks to Blackjack.

Would the world know FedEx today had Fred lost that $5000?

Who knows, perhaps he would have found another way through but this example shows that some household names almost never happened and that if you have a strong belief in your brand and know that beneath the bad timing lies a truly promising core that just needs that final extra boost to ignite, you will fight to the brink of survival to make it happen. Never give up too soon, never go down without a fight.

---

'Many of life's failures are people who did not realize how close they were to success when they gave up.'
*Thomas Edison*

---

But if you do pull success from the jaws of failure, don't get complacent. Whatever you do to keep the lights on, you'll need to do it for a while. The best things in life may be free but everything costs money and no matter how plump and promising they look, acorns always take lots of work to become oaks.

Look at the Statue of Liberty with her light aloft, the original girlboss of "Brand America"—standing proud with grandeur, permanence and grace.

But she didn't appear on that pedestal by magic. And truth be known, she almost didn't appear at all.

Getting her up was a long and drawn-out process fraught with financial problems from the outset. Constructing a 150-foot copper statue and shipping it from France to America was never cheap at the best of times, but in 1870 the prospect must have appeared ridiculous and impossible. To generate the funds necessary took time, patience,

* that's $87 ***billion.***

innovation, and nerve. In fact, at one point in 1876, the statue's torch-bearing arm was exhibited, on its own, at the Centennial Exposition in Philadelphia to raise money for the statue's further construction.

This must have been an arresting sight—but because this was before TV news and the internet, no matter how arresting it was, it wouldn't have been seen outside Philadelphia, apart from in the odd photograph, and so the arm was then hauled another hundred miles up to New York to be exhibited in Madison Square Garden for another six years, to generate the necessary investment. It was early crowd-sourcing.

But in 1882 investing in French-made public art projects wasn't high on the average New Yorker's To Do list, so the arm and its as-yet-unconstructed dismembered body were living on borrowed time. Had it not been for the publisher Joseph Pulitzer—who captured the public imagination with a campaign he ran in his newspaper New York World—the statue's copper could quite easily have been sold and repurposed as roofing material.

It's a good idea to start small and make money from the beginning, so you can scale up and use your brand to build your brand.

Branding is a leverage tool that can be used from the outset to optimise everything. When building a strong foundation for your brand, early planning allows you to identify and avoid many potential problems before they arise, so you can make subtle adjustments and iterations every step of the way.

With Give yourself a brand, you can do the major groundwork before you make any significant financial expense.

The first significant financial investment phase of the GYAB process is the creation of your primary identity, and by that time you will have actually authored a good portion of the brief you will need to give your graphic designer for that phase. Plus, you'll be in a much more confident position by that point to appraise both your brand's viability and your commitment levels.

---

'It's not about your resources,
it's about your resourcefulness.'
*Tony Robbins*

---

## Be Flawsome

As the notorious Catalonian surrealist Salvador Dali once said 'Have no fear of perfection—you'll never reach it.' So relax, kids, you don't have to be perfect.

Life is a constant series of flaws and potential flaws. But of course, they don't really exist in some sense. Not if you reframe them. Big problems are usually obvious but many "flaws" are quite subjective.

It's like the story of the old man, the boy, and the donkey who went to the market. They started off with the old man riding the donkey until a passer-by said 'Huh, making the boy walk, you should be ashamed of yourself!' And so they swapped until another passer-by said 'Huh! making the old man walk, you should be ashamed of yourself!' So they both got on until someone said 'How disgusting, that poor donkey!' And so they both decided to walk alongside the donkey, and when they got to market everyone fell about laughing, shouting 'What idiot has a donkey and doesn't use it?'

No matter your arrangements there will always be someone who says you're doing it wrong. You can't please all the people all the time.

So you have to act in accordance with—and in the direction of—certain key goals, key goals we will explore and outline in the following sections. If something you do directly serves these goals, then you're on track. However, if an event occurs that does not serve these goals, it should be taken seriously. And you should obviously try to fix it.

But what if some things just keep on going wrong? What if who you are, or the situation you are in, just keeps throwing up the same unresolvable problem?

In such cases, I might recommend you work with it.

Let the problem guide you. In embracing your flaw, you may find new value or an unseen niche.

What at first could appear as a "limitation" could be seen as inspiration towards a better course of action. Budget constraints often make better stories.

When Steven Spielberg was making the film Jaws, he had initially intended to make more use of three purpose-built animatronic sharks, collectively known as 'Bruce', to create authentic-looking shark attack scenes but...

...the animatronic sharks were unwieldy and temperamental and kept going wrong, delaying the shoot. Did Steven let this one major problem ruin the project? Did he say 'Oh that'll do, no one will notice the shark is a model and just let out some smoke'? Did he spend all his time and energy slagging off the model-making team? Did he give up and go home?

No. Steven quickly reverted to Plan B and used other techniques that suggested the presence of the shark, such as contextualising shots of the open sea, a barrel being dragged through the water, and camera POVs from the water level. And when all this was taken into the editing room and set against that stark world-famous John Williams soundtrack daa da daa da—it created a staggering effect. Thanks to Steven's attitude and working style, the technical problems helped transform what could have been a forgettable B-movie into a thrilling cinematic masterpiece.

Work with your problems, they could be gifts in disguise.

Sara Blakely was a woman who had a particular problem with 'visible panty lines' and struggled to find a solution. In doing so, she created the global brand Spanx.

Joanne Kathleen was a single mother facing huge problems, living on welfare and struggling with money and isolation. Instead of letting these issues deter her, she channelled them into the magical world of Harry Potter and became JK Rowling.

Harland Sanders saw great misfortune in his early life, losing jobs, going bankrupt, and failing several times before he went on to create KFC.

Richard Branson was dyslexic but created Virgin.

Howard Schultz grew up in poverty but created Starbucks.

And Walt Disney was fired from a newspaper job for lacking imagination!

In business and branding, attitude is your best friend. We are humans, and nobody's perfect. If you can't make mistakes in life, when can you? If you don't fail, you don't learn. Success is a poor teacher. But at some point you need success, it is worth aiming for. So where possible fix your flaws, but if you can't fix them, reframe them, work with them, see them as gifts, and become flawsome.

'If plan A fails, remember there are 25 more letters.'
*Chris Guillebeau*

## Earn your spotlight

'Daddy,' spat the young mosquito, 'everywhere I go I get nothing but applause.'

'No, Son,' spoke his father, 'they are trying to kill you.'

This cautionary tale is worth recalling when you're starting out with a new brand or business idea and telling everyone about it. Most reactions will be polite and difficult to pull actual value from. If you're trying to gauge genuine interest in your offerings then it's best to gauge that in a more compelling way. Use methods that garner actual data like a registration page or trial period. Encouragement and validation are obviously very welcomed when you're starting out but do take the time to discern genuine praise from fake stuff, if you can. Most people do not care about your brand. Sounds harsh but believe me, it's true.

In human psychology we have this thing called the "Spotlight Effect", and this means we walk around under our own little "spotlights" with the illusion other people are interested in us. But unless they are emotionally or financially involved on some level, they could not care less.

Entrepreneurs' networks—or similar support groups—can be helpful and highly valuable watering holes that give you much-needed encouragement and advice, but brutal honesty is usually quite rare in face-to-face interactions and this can blind you to the actual level of interest your brand garners, out there, in the real world.

Out there—"among the people"—do exist your future end-users, people who will, one day soon I hope find you but don't expect them to beat a hasty path to your door the minute you upload your website.

You can build it, and still, they won't come.

And if they do come, genuinely interested, don't expect smiles or praise. As any car salesperson will tell you, if someone's interested in buying: it's "PokerFace" all the way. If you're looking to buy something, you mostly don't flatter the offering unless you're trying to politely decline. If we want to buy, we usually assume the appearance of a cold fish and feign indifference to achieve a better negotiating position to bring that price down.

---

'We never get accustomed to being less important
to other people than they are to us.'
*Graham Greene*

---

## Give yourself time, like a great white shark...

Building your brand will take a while. You need to commit to it for the long haul. Be realistic. If someone asks you to build Rome, don't promise it back for end-of-play. Branding is "considered consistency" of Abilities, Content, and Touchpoints over time, and it can take twenty years to become an overnight success—if you're lucky.

Just keep swimming. Like the 'world's largest predatory fish', your friend and mine: the great white shark. They may move slowly—at typical cruising speeds rarely exceeding two or three miles an hour—but they never stop moving, ever. And so can travel up to 50 miles a day, every day. And a shark can move very fast if they need to, but only when they *really* need to. There's no point wasting energy on pointless haste. You don't see sharks being "busy" for the sake of it because their boss is in the room.

---

'Patience attracts happiness,
it brings near that which is far.'
*Swahili Proverb*

---

## ...beware perfectionism...

When building a brand, it's important to distinguish between the work that needs doing and stuff that doesn't.

Releasing new work—and putting yourself and your creations out into the world—can invite ridicule and punishment. Humanity is, after all, a cascading ecosystem of feedback loops. So we fret and fluster and over-prepare, erecting unnecessary barriers. We hesitate, defer, and excuse ourselves, but we can't do that forever otherwise our headstones will read: 'Dear beloved friend, who never did anything but if they had it would have been perfect.'

Perfectionism is especially damaging if you work alone, with only yourself as the sole arbiter of quality and reason, without the encouragement or guidance of other people.

And so, where possible, try to find your own feedback loops. Test what you have made with a close circle who can guide you with honest feedback. Asking for feedback from others—and outsourcing quality assurance—to invite opinions beyond your own head, is pretty much always a good idea. Most brands actively do this on some level, either with internal feedback loops between teams, client reviews, or focus groups or by releasing beta versions of their products and services.

Shape it, test it, ship it. 'Get ship done!' if you will.

## ...and choose quality over quantity

A good line gets repeated. A good video gets shared. A good hat makes a good photo. A good photo is chosen by an editor or art director and makes the magazine. A good product gets talked about. Good packaging gets more shelf space. Bar managers stick a bottle of Tia Maria on the well-lit shelves to say 'You want class? We do class. Look, Tia Maria.' Tia Maria invested in good product development (a key Ability) but it also invested in good branding and created a complete "world" people could buy into. Tia Maria is not just a beverage, it's an experience. An experience dripping with meaning and association. And its name, identity, style, packaging, and marketing all reinforce this "World of Experience". Get your world right before you increase the size of your world.

That's the key to attracting fans.

If you want a very big fire, you don't slightly warm up a very big region, you concentrate on one small area with a highly focused point of heat. If you want to be "Big in Japan" you don't slightly please a huge population of people, rather you win the intense affection of a tight clique of super-fans. Quality before quantity.

---

'Most of us have two lives.
The life we live, and the unlived life within us.
Between the two stands Resistance.'
*Steven Pressfield (The War of Art)*

---

## ORATErs gonna ORATE

There is a widely-used principle in marketing called AIDA and brands use this acronym as a guide for creating communications that cut through and convert their prospects. It recommends that an action, advert, or communication must generate Awareness, then Interest, to create Desire, which inspires Action. A.I.D.A. Which works well enough.

However, I have made a slight update to this. I have incorporated the key aspect of Trust and I have changed Action to Engagement—a subtle but important difference—and I have created the O.R.A.T.E. system:
Observance, Realisation, Aspiration, Trust, and Engagement.

The audience must first <u>Observe</u> your brand or its value offering, then they must <u>Realise</u> it is relevant to them, which makes them <u>Aspire</u> to proceed, and in order to go further the prospect must <u>Trust</u> the proposition, she may then <u>Engage</u>. This applies to all your brand's content and touchpoints. AIDA and ORATE are effective sequences to consider.

No matter how amazing a brand is, if no one observes its existence, it will not go anywhere. If people do not realise why a brand's offering could be relevant or valuable to them, they will not aspire to proceed. If they do not trust you, it's game over, forget about engagement.

Someone buying a book is a great example of the ORATE process. Observance is when we notice the book's name or front cover, it stands out and catches our eye. Realisation is where we see it is a subject or author we're likely to enjoy or get benefit from. Aspiration can then arise in the heart of the prospective reader, provided they like what they're seeing, and so they now want to proceed, but they are cautious. Trust is only won after the potential buyer has checked all the clues: the word count, the reviews and recommendations, and the price. They may even smell the paper. And when they have satisfied these four steps they can then, and only then, take the final step. Engagement is never guaranteed but if it does come, it comes at the end of this process and rarely before trust is won.

This process can be applied to every aspect of branding. You need to be seen and seen as relevant before a fan will want what you're offering and you need to be trusted before a fan will engage.

---

'Your brand is its Abilities, its Content, its Touchpoints, its Offerings, and its Signposts. Together these create more value than the sum of their parts. But only if your end-user ORATEs you. Your brand needs to be Observed, Realised as relevant, Aspired towards, and Trusted, to be Engaged with.'
*Luke Arwen Shaw*

---

## Start small, stay grounded, stay hungry, outsource where possible, and give yourself hope

### It's ok to start small, as long as you start

No matter how grand your vision, when you start off, you'll probably need to start small, with what you have.

You may aspire to be the next Disney or the next HP Inc., as big as IKEA, or Dyson. However, at first, your resources will naturally be limited. So you may not have enough money to get a proper premises or store or workshop. You might even have to make do with a garage or a garden shed.

However, the wonderful thing about branding is that it can be used to add leverage to your work, and you can use your brand to build your brand.

---

'You don't have to be great to start,
but to be great ... you *do* have to start.'
*Zig Ziglar*

---

### It's important to stay grounded

The only reason we are here is because our mums had sex with our dads. Remember that the next time you get flustered about your status, popularity, or so-called success rates. And remember that everyone everywhere, no matter their place in life was once a helpless baby and remember that everyone is going to die and after we die we will start to smell bad within a few days, unless properly treated.

We are biological, and vulnerable, and limited.

But it's not all bad ... your entire ancestral line has survived, intact. For quite a while. Not for a week, not a year, but the last three and a half billion years!

Despite incalculable levels of incredible danger, and cataclysm, ice ages, famines, wars, and GDPR ('yes, I accept cookies!'), every single one of your ancestors not only survived to sexual maturity but produced the offspring that led to you. Ever since the seemingly random point in time, when life somehow miraculously emerged on Earth. And only because all the elements necessary to make that miracle happen came from stars exploding millions of miles away, millions of years before that. So while it's tempting to turn around and say, 'I and I alone made that Cornish pasty!' the truth is, you got lucky.

So stay grounded.

Never lose connection with those around you.

Never lose connection with those you serve and work with.

To maintain relevance on the street, you need to constantly seek ways of grounding your brand. IKEA produces furniture for humans and it takes the work of listening to and learning about, the lives of those it serves.

Just like the US comedians Dave Chapelle and Chris Rock, who write their arena Specials by engaging with small rooms throughout the preceding years, IKEA stays grounded through on-the-ground research, feedback, and constant connection with its audience, to ensure it can iterate its offerings and grow authentically.

## It's important to stay hungry

One reason why you may want to give yourself a brand is to do something new to create something successful so you can finally relax.

However, new soon becomes normal and a success loses its novelty after about a week. To stay motivated, you need to kill complacency, you need to keep your eyes on a bigger prize, and never forget where you are going and why you're going there. Basically, you need to stay hungry, Girlfriend.

But how? What do you do when new becomes normal? You search. And you keep searching, for "new new". You pioneer. You push new boundaries, bring in new initiatives, play with new ideas, keep things fresh, and keep things moving.

Look at HP Inc., previously called Hewlett-Packard.

Its founders, Bill Hewlett and David Packard*, started working together in 1938 and quickly found success with their designs and products. One of the first designs they successfully patented was a precision audio oscillator. I'll be honest, I don't know what one of

* Bill and David flipped a coin to see which way around their names would go, meaning we could be talking about the PH brand today.

these is—I think it's a device that measures sound frequencies—but I do know they were very popular, and even Disney used them during the production of Fantasia.

Bill and Dave could have just kept making these popular precision audio oscillators—they could have been the top name in precision audio oscillators— but no, they stayed hungry and pressed on. Bill had to do a bit of army time but soon returned to move HP into a new headquarters on Palo Alto's Page Mill Road in 1940, where they stayed hungry and got into the microwave game, ahead of their future leadership in signal generators. Throughout the 1940s they grew and grew with their dedication to making 'products that would make a difference for their customers', but also taking care of their employees with a health insurance plan which was rare for its day. And as they moved through the 1950s they went public, and just before the 1960s they went global. Throughout the 1960s they stayed hungry and entered the medical field with their ethos of innovation, growth, and quality and found themselves listed by Fortune as the 460th most powerful company in America.

They stayed hungry and introduced progressive working methods and recreational facilities for their teams, creating what could be called 'the birth of Palo Alto culture', a culture that today has spawned Google, Facebook, Tesla, VMware, and Quora among many others.

HP stayed hungry throughout the 1970s, 1980s, and 1990s and made a very successful transition into the 21st Century becoming one of the world's largest IT brands. In 2023 HP Inc. had 58,000 employees, a global net revenue of over $53 billion a year, and held over 22,000 patents. *That* is staying hungry.

## Outsource, wherever you can

Do you think Walt Disney did every drawing himself?

'Would you turn the telly down! I'm trying to finish Fantasia up here!'

You cannot do everything yourself.

Save up some money or get some initial capital. Then do work and get people to help you. Sell the result of that work and you pay the people who helped you. It isn't a ground-breaking concept but it does require care and attention. You must find appropriate people—and have the ability to pay them, which can be a balancing act—but the key advantage of this system is that you can scale and grow beyond your own limited time and resources. The key tension—or challenge—with scaling is the flipside of this same coin. That is to say, the bigger you become the more complex your brand becomes and potentially the slower it is to react and adapt to change. And that's why you must scale at rates that match—or slightly presume—the demand for your offerings.

Outsource-based scaling becomes so much easier when you have a brand.

Having a brand, and branded ecosystem, in place, enables you to own every Touchpoint and gateway. Again, the flipside to this advantage—of marking your territory and claiming ownership—is that when you release control of your Abilities, Content, and Touchpoints to others, your brand runs the risk of being associated with poor quality. And because your brand is only as strong as its weakest link—you must ensure you take responsibility for quality assurance (QA) and ensure those you employ or outsource to are a good fit.

However, outsourcing is the key to scaling your brand and is necessary for achieving success.

Yes, it can take a while to develop such an ecosystem into being, but that's where your brand will help you. The more you can outsource to others, the more you can do what it is you do best.

## It's important to give yourself hope

The Dyson brand—known for putting bagless vacuum cleaners in our homes and airblade hand dryers in our public toilets—was created by James Dyson. His brand is world-famous for its innovative futuristic technology and revolutionary products that I can't imagine living life without.

But James didn't achieve the finished design for his bagless vacuum cleaner over breakfast. It wasn't done in a week. It wasn't even done in a year. Or five years. Or ten. It took fifteen.

Fifteen *years*.

And James didn't just knock out the first prototype and think, 'yeah, that'd do.' He kept perfecting it and perfecting it. Was he being a perfectionist? No. He wasn't inventing unnecessary work, he was just inventing something that had to work. Difficult, uncharted work.

Solving a complicated problem without a manual. He was pioneering; creating a truly innovative design that no one had created before. And there's nowhere to hide with product design, you can't gloss over a flaw. Products get stress-tested to failure and need to go the distance.

No product will ever be absolutely perfect for every end-user but the product has to work and work safely. It has to honour its proposition, it has to keep its promise. And so James kept on developing, producing prototype after prototype. Even though the whole time he had expenses, responsibilities, and mouths to feed.

And after three and a half thousand prototypes: James still did not have a bagless vacuum cleaner he was satisfied with.

Did he give up? Did he let the intense pressure of his financial difficulties force him to pursue another path? No, he gave himself hope. Eventually—15 years after his original idea, having completed 5,127 prototypes—James finally had a design he was happy with.

And even then it wouldn't sell.

It wouldn't sell because the whole vacuum cleaning sales model was based on bags. It was the bags that made the money—a bit like the razor blade business model. So potential sales partners—like vacuum cleaner sellers—were having none of it. No one would license his bagless cleaner. No one would agree to make the thing in sufficient numbers. This essentially shut down his plan to find a licensing deal in the US. But James gave himself hope and finally found a small licensing company able to help him find a willing manufacturer. However, the manufacturing deal required the bagless cleaner be made only in 'pastel pink', sold only in Japan, and retailed only at $2000 per product—not the most obvious path to ensuring worldwide success.

After all this hard work was his grand idea going to end up somewhere as an obscure museum exhibit, covered in ironic dust?

No.

James gave himself more hope and he went for it, securing his first commercially available vacuum, produced under license by the Japanese company Apex Inc., in 1986.

And in 1991 his pink plastic Dual Cyclone design won the prestigious International Design Fair award in Tokyo. This plaudit, together with the massive popularity his cleaner received from the Japanese market, inspired and allowed James to start up the Dyson company in 1993.

The entire time from 1978—when he originally fell in love with the idea of a bagless cleaner—right up to 1993, James gave himself hope and it paid off.

Yes, it took more than hope. It took energy, hard work, intelligence, guts, grit, creativity, courage, and perseverance but without hope, you cannot harness what you need to go forward.

Was all the hope worth it? Did it turn out ok?

Today James is known as Sir James Dyson and has an estimated net worth of around $4.6 billion.

You need to believe in yourself, and your idea—if you don't believe in your brand, no one else will. You really do need to hope your brand will turn out ok, and as we see time and again, it always helps to be big in Japan.

'Hope' is a dirty word in business—with everyone pushing metrics, hyper-targeting, and shutting things down if they don't yield an immediate return on investment—but in life, hope is all you've got.

---

'If you don't give up, you still have a chance.'
*Jack Ma*

---

Few people have a super positive inner voice—but we have so much potential, so we just need to stay hopeful to keep going. We must find the hope, tools, and inspiration to keep walking, daily, into the unknown.

Because one day, it will pay off. At least, that's the hope.

Any creative venture is a constant dance between doubt and belief, disillusionment and inspiration, struggle and relaxation so here's where we relax a bit and believe in ourselves. Great brands differ in name and identity and style and voice and offering, but at heart, they share much in common. Great brands stay grounded, stay hungry, outsource where possible, and give themselves and their audiences hope. And do you know another thing that Disney, HP Inc., IKEA, and Dyson have in common?

All four started out in either a garage or a garden shed.

# Part 3

# Give your brand a foundation

Follow the next eight steps and you will build an authentic brand with a strong foundation, ready for a rich life of ACTivity.

Let's get this party started.

**STEP 1**

# Give your brand a why

What is your **reason-for-being**?

## What is a why and why do you need one?

You need a why.

Do not underestimate the value of your whys.

I know many of us venture out each day with a devil-may-care strut of fatalistic panache, 'We can leave it to chance, George. Que sera. See what happens. Let the universe surprise us!'

Which is fine but I have a question: are you wearing clothes today when you leave the house?

What's that? Yes?

You didn't leave it to chance?

No. Of course, you didn't. You didn't bound naked onto the street saying 'I'm sure the clothes will just turn up somewhere ... I'll let the universe surprise us!'

You're wearing clothes because you had a strong reason to dress before leaving the house, and that reason gave you a mission and you executed that mission like you were Chuck Norris ... it gave you a strong why. A goal. An overarching quest.

'Cos strong whys get results.

You have loads of little whys that guide your day. A hundred little reasons that guide your successful daily actions. You lift the kettle, release the handbrake, type the letters, wave at the postman, and follow the good guidance of a hundred little meaningful whys that work wonders.

However, it's likely you don't have a Super Why.

I put it to you, dear reader, that you don't have a big solid juicy reason-for-being that you can pull out and slap on the table.

Oh, sure, you may have some vague objectives: be nice, make money, be loyal—but the problem with vague objectives is they're vague. Wishy-washy. Vague objectives don't really inspire and lock you to meaningful and focused action driven towards a well-defined end goal that excites you. You don't have a big why.

Well, I think it's about time you got one.

Because a super why gives you rocket fuel and a destination to aim for. If you wish to give yourself a brand, you must start with the why, the reason why your brand needs to exist. This why will be vital to keep you focused and motivated. To silence the short-term alarms and distractions and excuses and sulking fits that constantly sap your energy and pull you off track.

If you visit ***giveyourselfabrand.com/findyourwhy*** you will be able to download a worksheet. And in that worksheet, you will find a series of statements that invite completion. Your answers to these will reveal your big why.

This is your ticket to visit "You Country"—a deep dive into who you are and what makes you tick. Treat each question, each revelation, and each discovery with time and care. Consider what it is you are seeing about yourself, about the work you wish to do and the brand you wish to create, and most importantly: the reasons why.

Just focus on what you want. There's only one rule: it can only be the good stuff, the stuff of your hopes and dreams, that stuff that makes your blood sing with joy. Silence everything else.

Why does a metal detector find the metal? Because it is focused, on metal. It's not bothered, or distracted by, the overwhelming sea of dirt in which it lies buried. If you bought a metal detector that constantly flapped on about how it was 'possibly missing a load of wood' you'd bin the thing.

Focus is value. And so you must use the following questions to hone in on what it is that drives and enlivens you. You'll start to see that real why that gently glows at the heart of your being—the 'overarching quest' that's been waiting with patience, for when you are ready to serve it.

You are unique, and you have a unique personality and a unique take on this world ... and you have unique potential—now you need to leverage that into an engine of action.

Now is the time to have some fun and find the things that make up who you are. Ignite yourself, so you can ignite others. Your why is the starting gun that will begin your journey and the laser beam that will guide that journey. A strong why provides you meaningful motivation, because it provides you with a strong need.

We all do what needs to get done.

We have more opportunities and resources available to us than ever before but the question is 'What do you want to do?'

When you find the answer, when you find your why—and you will find it—accept your why. And give it a little hug. Don't regret not finding it sooner, it probably didn't exist in the world before you decided to look for it.

Life's funny like that.

All those things that happened in your life? Use them to be the best you.

Your entire life has led up to this point where you now create and serve your big why best. And you will serve it, and it will serve you. It will give you the idea, the desire, the meaning, the permission, the motivation, and the focus you are going to need to give yourself a brand—so what are you waiting for?

---

'The two most important days in your life are the day you are born and the day you find out why.'
*Mark Twain*

---

**Find your big why by downloading the worksheet at: giveyourselfabrand.com/findyourwhy**

**STEP 2**

# Give your brand an ethos

What is your **way-of-being**?

## What is an ethos and why do you need one?

An ethos is a belief system.

It's your brand's approach to life. The credo. The code. The golden thread that runs through your brand.

'Right,' yawns Uncle Brian, waking from his nap, 'so, is an ethos the definitive articulation of the values that will guide and inspire you?'

Yes, Brian. Correct.

'Ok,' he frowns, 'why on Earth would I need one of those?'

So you can build a brand in line with your values, Brian.

If you consider this step well and follow your ethos over time, good things will happen.

I promise you.

In the last section, we defined your why, and you downloaded the worksheet and wrote out what really drives you and where you're driving to. Remember?

Well, dear reader, now that you know roughly where you're going, we need to agree on how you're getting there.

So you can reach your destination in the best way possible.

And it will also help you attract others to travel with you.

'But why are values relevant in branding?' asks Uncle Brian, 'Isn't branding more about logos, fabrics, and wallpaper? Shouldn't we be focusing on Whats and Things? Rather than airy-fairy sentiments?

Look out there, Brian. Look at all the Whats and Things we're trying so hard to get. The logos, the fabrics, the wallpaper. The house, the home, the shoes, the hair, the shirt, the skirt, the flag, the swag. The Gucci glasses, Prada purse, and high-spec German sports car with its reassuringly heavy key fob. The football boots, the business suits, and Robertson's Golden Shred. The Sprinter van, the spray-on tan, and Beats by Dr Dre (and floral dresses by Diane von Furstenberg).

Now look again, Brian, and look closer this time, and you'll see that each thing, each product or service, represents something more than the thing itself.

The thing is nothing but an expression of values.

A Porsche is not just a car, it's an assertion of craftsmanship, and creative prowess, and the beauty that can be achieved with grease and spanners. A designer dress is not just a designer dress, it's a declaration of grace, and hope, or dissent, in the face of an often ugly and oppressive world. A marmalade is not just a sugar-laden toast topping, but a deep acknowledgment to the earth or to our grandmother and all she believed in. Even a cut-price bog roll stands for something. The health and cleanliness of those it hopes to serve.

A "thing" is a connection to something beyond ourselves. Products and services are simply expressions of what the makers and their end-users *value*, be that pet food, pillows, or private jets.

'Shut up,' sneers Uncle Brian, 'as you said yourself, people don't really want your brand, they only really want what your brand can do for them. So you just need to fulfil their needs.'

Yes, Brian, but do not underestimate how much people look to brands on an interpersonal level, to help them fulfil deep-seated psychological needs. People want to feel connected to the world, and connected in a way that works harmoniously with their emotional needs.

We use things to help us do this.

Cars are a great example of how much people use brands to define their sense of identity.

'I can only drive a Honda, George, and you would never catch me in a BMW.'

'Yes,' scoffs Uncle Brian, 'only 'cos she cant afford it.'

Not so fast, Brian, do not underestimate Aunty Deborah's sense of identity. Do not underestimate just how far BMWs feel from her personal realm of being, and how much she sees them as living manifestations of 'those types of people'.

Now, Deborah is no expert and she does not know what, if any, mechanical differences exist between her Honda and the BMW next door. But she knows she's not a BMW driver. And she will sneer at those who drive them but she'd probably rather a BMW driver gave her daughter a lift if she was ever stricken by the roadside in need of a samaritan because Deborah believes BMW drivers are aloof, arrogant, and lacking in certain virtues but they are trustworthy.

In human societies, people build rulebooks of meaning to help them navigate their lives, and central to these psychological frameworks are values ... those airy-fairy sentiments, Brian.

Values are the subtle, unseen conductors of human action and at the end of the day, we value values more than profit, more than things, more than life itself.

And we use things—products, services, stories—as tools to challenge, or transform, ourselves inside our governing set of values.

'This is who I am, George! This is what I need!'

Anyone can Observe and Realise the relevance of your brand—provided they see a demonstration of your Abilities, usually via your Content and Touchpoints—but it's only when they see that you share the same values as them, that they Aspire to use your brand for the long-term.

People don't care how much you know until they know how much you care.

If someone perceives you to share the same values, they will feel closer to you and be more trusting of you.

And your brand will grow.

But the bigger your brand gets, the harder it becomes to curate every last Touchpoint, and a brand is only as strong as its weakest link. So, without a golden thread running through it, the whole system can lose its way and come unstuck.

If someone feels you have breached their values, they will get angry, and in the commercial world, that can be disastrous. It doesn't take much to please people, but it doesn't take much to anger them either. You can use the best designers, architects, and suppliers to attract a customer worth £1000 a year to your coffee shop, but all it takes is one angry barista to lose that customer forever. 'Come on, George, we're leaving.'

A nice smile can be worth thousands.

---

'If people believe they share values
with a company, they will stay loyal
to the brand.'
*Howard Shultz*

---

Whether you keep your ethos private or public, it's important to share it where possible among those who will be responsible for expressing—and acting on behalf of—your brand, to ensure everyone batting for your team is following the same guiding values.

Our world is ultimately a trading post of values, where we, in our own ways, share what it means to be human.

'What it means, to me, to be a mechanic','What it means to us, to campaign for the protection of wildlife.'

Good values are good branding and good values are good for business.

If your brand can give its audience the transformations it seeks, in a way that aligns with its values, your brand will be successful.

---

'Overall, because branding is about creating and sustaining trust it means delivering on promises. The best and most successful brands are completely coherent. Every aspect of what they do and what they are reinforces everything else.'
*Wally Olins*

---

‘I’m still not sure, you know,’ frowns Uncle Brian, ‘this whole values ethos manifesto business sounds like some kind of cult. A brand is a business, mate. It’s not a religion or a socio-political movement, and anyway, I’m not even sure you need one.’

Ok, Brian. I take your concerns on board but if I may, let me finish up with a little story about a man called Mr Yoshida. You may not have heard of him but he saw the value in an ethos. He started up a company in 1934 in Tokyo, Japan.

‘Was it big?’

So so. The company was a modest operation specialising in the manufacture of a particular product. But the point here is that very early on, Mr Yoshida defined and articulated his set of values and beliefs in how one should provide value. After much thought and reflection, he created an ethos that could be translated as ‘The Cycle of Goodness’ which said ‘No one prospers unless he renders benefits to others.’

Mr Yoshida used this guiding principle, or ethos, to unite people and guide the efforts needed to build his company.

‘What company?’

It could be translated as Yoshida Industries Limited, but it’s a Japanese operation so it was called Yoshida Kogyo Kabushikikaisha, but in 1994 the name was shortened. And what products does this brand make? Zips and zip fasteners. Right now—no matter where you’re reading this—you are either wearing one of his zips or you’re very close to one. YKK has become one of the most wide-reaching brands in human history.

---

‘It’s not hard to make decisions when
you know what your values are.’
*Roy Disney*

---

A good ethos:

– is a reminder of what is important

– gives you direction when things are confusing, and helps you and your people weather the steep curves that often beset fledgling businesses

– bonds people whose viewpoints differ outside your brand and shows them they do in fact share belief overlaps and points of consensus

– reduces conflict

– provides a means of finding resolutions if disputes arise

– creates conditions for a safe and supportive culture of opportunity where everyone knows the rules, and can achieve the best results without confusion or micromanagement

– works with your Why of your brand to capture compelling reasons for the existence of your brand and helps inform your strategic intent

– gets the baker a long line at his door, the florist invited to every wedding in town, and the barista a coffee shop full of happy customers.

In writing an ethos for your brand, you create an opportunity to lay down the principles that resonate with your highest inner knowing so you can become a "leader brand".

You can show others how you want to do business.

## How do you define and articulate your ethos?

You know your values. No one knows your values better than you. But you may have never actually sought to think about them too much or write them down in any way.

It's worth doing.

The first step is to look at—and answer—the questions you will find by downloading the worksheet for this section.

The worksheet will help think about what it is you value and what you can do to make these values better influence your work.

'Why would I want to do that?'

Think about it. You'll see it's worth doing. When you act in alignment with your values, you'll sleep at night, you'll rise with enthusiasm, and you'll be able to deal with everything that life throws at you.

If you visit *giveyourselfabrand.com/findyourethos* you will be able to download a worksheet. In that worksheet, you will find a series of questions to help you create a succinct statement that best describes your brand's ethos.

## Create your ethos by downloading the worksheet at: giveyourselfabrand.com/findyourethos

**STEP 3**

# Give your brand an end-user

**Who** do you serve and transform?

## What is an end-user and why do you need one?

It's time to think about your brand's end-user.

'What's an end-user?'

An end-user is the person who is going to want, and use, the offerings your brand supplies.

There can be no supply without demand.

So, you now know your why and your ethos; you know where your brand is going and how it's getting there

Now it's time to think about who your brand will serve.

We know why you're giving yourself this brand, we know in what way your brand will conduct itself but now we need to know who is going to appreciate that.

It's time to "find your tribe".

It's time to create the profile of your end-user because without one there can be no brand.

Imagine a brand called Cheekipop.

Cheekipop loves to make fruit juice and juice-related products and distributes them across stores nationwide. It loves doing this, it's so enthusiastic about juice.

But oranges and lemons, bottling plants, and staff, all cost money. So if Cheekipop wants to make fruit juice and juice-related products and distribute them across stores nationwide, it must use its enthusiasm, and intelligence, to find and create an actual fan base of end-users.

A fanbase that likes and actually buys its products. Cheekipop must sell products to make more products.

It's a cycle.

Cheekipop's end-user most likely does not buy directly from Cheekipop HQ. With fast-moving consumer goods (FMCGs) like Cheekipop, there's usually a chain involved.

The brand's product is produced, packaged, and distributed from its origination plant and supplied to distribution partners like supermarkets and wholesalers, who either redistribute the pallets of poly-wrapped Cheekipop to smaller stores or sell to independent store owners. These smaller supermarkets and independent stores then sell Cheekipop directly to Cheekipop's end-users. This is vital; the end-user is key.

Sales of Cheekipop determine Cheekipop's future.

Sales are influenced by several factors—branding, product, marketing, location, merchandising, weather—but ultimately, if no one buys Cheekipop, Cheekipop must change or die.

If Cheekipop takes the time to think about—and research—what its end-user wants, it can direct its branding, packaging, product development, and marketing, to best suit and serve that end-user on the street, and create demand.

If Cheekipop does its homework—its end-user will buy.

If the end-user buys Cheekipop, the store will want Cheekipop. If the store wants Cheekipop, the wholesaler will want Cheekipop. If the wholesaler wants Cheekipop, then that is just Cheekipop-tastic.

Good commerce is simply a conversation between the one who supplies and the one who demands. It's that universal law of exchange.

There is a supply chain involved but ultimately the important aspect is the conversation between a brand and its end-user. This conversation maintains the demand, the chain, and the virtuous life cycle.

Defining your end-user helps you find your end-user.

You are my end-user. There have been various stages between me writing these words and you receiving them. Others have been involved in the chain. Someone had to edit everything, check the spelling, and design the layout of the pages. Someone had to pour ink into a printer and bind and trim the pages. But ultimately it's between me and you. If I please you, I can continue. If I don't please you, I must change or die.

So do I know who you are? Have I researched *you*—as my end-user?

Of course.

And I know you:

- have an interest in branding and/or creating your own brand
- like to be spoken to with consideration
- are intelligent, brilliant, and fantastic
- want relevant information and guidance, to better inform your decisions so you can live your best life.

To be fair, it's quite a short list, but there's no point in adding needs and virtues for the sake of it. After all, with every added virtue you add, you add yet another parameter that limits your pool of end-users. This can of course be valuable in identifying rich niches, but the best end-user profiles are detail-oriented without being too restrictive.

I will also develop separate end-user profiles for sales and marketing reasons. And for this, I will leverage social media. I will use my website and blog to see where certain pages and articles appear to resonate with a particular audience. I will use email marketing and collaborate with peers, influencers, and thought leaders where possible. All in an IKEA-like learning process to see where my fans are, and what it is they want. What they really, really want.

Whatever it is you are selling, a good grasp of who your ideal end-user is, enables you to see where, and when, you can best reach that ideal end-user.

Later, we will look at how to make your Abilities, Content, and Touchpoints attract, transform, and retain your end-users—but before you do that we need to define your end-user. Because the better you know who you're serving, the better you can serve.

Imagine you are invited to a party only to find stale cheesy puffs on paper plates, a host who doesn't know your name and isn't quite sure if you should be there, nowhere to put your coat, no one who speaks your language, a cash-only bar with limited stock and sour-faced bar staff. Would you feel in the mood for 'party party'? Or would you leave?

Defining your end-user helps you please your end-user.

Your job is to please both your end-user and yourself. 100%.

If you are not 100% enthusiastic about what you offer, you'll be overtaken by a competitor who is. If your end-users are not 100% enthusiastic about your offerings, your offerings won't sell and you will fail to create the necessary life cycle.

When your big why meets another person's "need", it's business time.

So who is your end-user? What transformations do they need? What are their values? What's their budget? What do they believe? What do they do? Where? With who? Why are they coming to your brand? What are they hoping to find?

If you're a hairdresser you may think... 'Look, I'm a hairdresser, Pet, I have a shop on the high street, why do I need to think about an end-user profile?'

Because it will enhance every aspect of your brand and help you create a suite of Touchpoints more attractive to those you wish to serve. Your end-user wants to be transformed. And if you can transform them—in a way that pleases them, that works for them, that they can afford, that aligns with their sense of identity and that adheres to their personal and tribal value codes—then you have a chance.

A chance to create a meaningful connection with your audience.

Ultimately, you need to use your ideas to transform people.

That's what good business is. And that's what good branding is.

People aren't really looking for 'products' or 'services', they're looking for transformations.

'Hang on,' sniffs Uncle Brian, 'I think people are looking for products. I went to B&Q last week because I wanted a power drill.'

No, Brian. You went to B&Q because you needed a hole. And a power drill is the best way of creating that hole.

When considering how to provide value to audiences, and seeing where you can disrupt existing markets and deliver new value, it pays to use first principles. Don't look at the scratch, look at the itch that causes the scratch.

Why does your end-user want the transformation?

They don't necessarily want the car for the sake of it, they want the freedom the car provides, inside their sense of identity. They don't want the cigarette per se, they want that moment of "space", peace, relief, and euphoria where they can be at one with themselves.

When you know why people do things, you can help them better. You can consider 'replacement therapies' for smokers, and you can generate options and alternatives for anything, because people mostly just want the effect a thing gives, rather than the thing itself.

Your brand exists to transform an end-user. It helps to see what is needed or desired and why it is needed or desired.

You don't buy a drill because you want a drill—no matter how much fun it is—you buy a drill because you want a hole. And you want that hole because you want a bookshelf. And you want the bookshelf to house your books. And you want books to transform yourself. Because your highest need is self-actualisation.* Bookshelves transform a house into a home. Champagne transforms a meal into a celebration. Paracetamol transforms an aching head. Food transforms the hungry into the capable. The burning of coal transforms thousands of years of decomposed and dehydrated vegetation into energy which is transformed into electricity which is transformed into heat which is

* According to Abraham Maslow's Hierarchy of needs.

transformed back into cold. All these transformations took place just because somebody wanted to participate in life, spend some quality time with their new spouse in their new home over a bank holiday weekend, and experience meaningful transformations that aligned with their sense of identity.

The more you know who your end-users are as people—and the more you know what pleases them—the more you can provide a branded world of offerings that your end-user loves.

---

'Build something 100 people love,
not something 1 million people kind of like.'
*Brian Chesky, co-founder of Airbnb*

---

## Who loves ya, Baby?

In the early days—before you've established yourself—it can feel like no one wants what you're offering, but remember: there are seven or so billion of us living on planet Earth, so there are always new opportunities.

Never underestimate the size of your potential audience. Everyone has an authentic fan club. Everyone. Everyone and everything is loved by someone.

Animal dung has a loving audience of admirers.

Flies.

A fly double-takes when it goes past a fresh animal dung, 'What? Someone's just thrown that away? Are they mad?'

We all want different things. The universe is designed that way.

If you concentrate foremost on your brand and your core offerings and focus on serving the needs of your end-users, you will achieve authentic and satisfying experiences for everyone involved.

Finding your best audience is a lot like detective work. From one piece of information, you can extrapolate (i.e. intelligently assume) other things. For example, if you have determined your end-user is a motorcyclist, then you can discover 'dependencies' (i.e. facts that follow from facts). If you know your end-user drives a motorbike, you can assume they require fuel, so you can safely predict they use petrol stations on a regular basis. When you create a detailed profile of your end-user, their needs—and their related needs—you can build up a richer picture of engagement opportunities.

Focusing first on an audience of one can help you find an audience of millions. From looking at the specifics and unique details of your end-users' lives, you can discover unmet needs and potential new offerings.

McDonald's Filet-O-Fish is a very popular item across the world selling in the US, Europe, India, Russia and, of course, it's big in Japan. However, this global favourite was developed to cater specifically to Catholic customers in Cincinnati, Ohio, who didn't eat meat during Lent. From identifying—and catering to—the unmet needs of one localised group, the brand was able to create a hit and roll it out to international acclaim.

## How do you find your end-user?

This chapter is not about actively attracting or retaining your end-user via means and methods such as marketing or Customer Relationship Management (CRM)—this chapter is about the early definition of your end-user so you can start to pave the way for your end-user attraction and retention.

Knowing who it is that you most want to serve will help you develop your brand foundation and your brand's Abilities, Content, and Touchpoints. There are many brilliant resources available such as HubSpot, Mailchimp, Salesforce.com, and many other online experts that can help you develop and manage your marketing and CRM systems—but before you start spending money on growing and interacting with lists of actual prospects and end-users, it's important to first define who those prospects and end-users are as people.

End-user profiling is a practice valuable for every A.C.T. performance your brand undertakes, at any point. However, in this, the foundational stage of building your brand, your end-user profile can be as wide or narrow as you wish. The Q&A section you will find in this section's worksheet (linked to overleaf) will allow you to think about who it is you wish to serve, so you can build a better brand foundation.

To give yourself a brand, you need to create an audience that loves your offering, uses your offering, and comes back for more—and tells others about it. If you visit giveyourselfabrand.com/findyourend-user you will be able to download a worksheet.

In that worksheet, you will find an opportunity to research, examine, and define your end-user. The worksheet has been designed to help you:

- visualise who it is you want to serve
- create a broad view of possible options
- create a definitive end-user profile.

Important and valuable to know and have ... after all, the entire process of any business can be distilled into just three fundamental points:

- Define end-user
- Find end-user
- Please end-user.

---

'There is only one winning strategy. It is to carefully define the target market and direct a superior offering to that target market.'
Philip Kotler.

---

**Create your end-user profile by downloading the worksheet at: giveyourselfabrand.com/findyourend-user**

## STEP 4

# Give your brand a name

What are we to **call** you?

## What is a name and why do you need one?

Your brand now needs a name. One that we hope will become much-loved and trusted the world over.

But what is a name and why do you need one?

A name is a word—or a set of words—that we humans use to create a referable entity. Naming things creates efficiency. Allows us to refer to things fast, with precision, and saves us from having to describe the thing each time.

Names enable us to tag, identify, and exchange all manner of information. 'Look at that OAK, ROBERT, listen to that JAZZ. Please get me some SALT & VINEGAR HULA HOOPS. And I want change.'

Whatever you're creating in your brand-building—a business, a product, a trifle—it must first be named, because everything starts with a name.

What's the first thing we do when we have a child?

We name it.

What's the first thing we do when we introduce ourselves to someone?

We start with our name, then run through other names, conversing, sharing nouns and ideas and reference points. 'Hello, I'm Luke, I come from planet Earth. Do you like Dark Wave? Oh, lovely, fancy a Cheekipop?'

In branding—like in life—names lead the way. They're incredibly valuable and can make or break your brand, being as they are the purest form of branding, the ultimate "digital asset".

And by that I mean they can be reproduced very cheaply, and quickly, and easily and effectively, for the cost of a human breath or a few keys on a keyboard or the dance of a biro ... and the better they are, the stickier they are, the more DURABLE they are, the more they will be reproduced, talked about, heard, remembered, shared, sought out and celebrated.

Names are valuable as functional handles—to herald and manoeuvre ideas—but they are also an opportunity to add further value to ideas through the power of association. Because these handles tap into the deep ocean of pre-established meanings we humans already have in our rich languages.

The trick is to find new ways of using words so you can create new entities. New entities that feel as though they've already existed in some way because they are created from pre-established words. So a good name is not only unique—and therefore protectable—but also trustworthy by virtue of its deep connection to a language we've all been speaking since birth.

Imagine a paint seller launches a new 'summer collection' range of colours: an off-white, a grey, a green, and a pink. If he were to stick those on the shelves with the names: Off-white, Grey, Green, and Pink, he would be a moron. There is, after all, more than one shade of grey. And imagine our reactions as customers, perusing the swatch chart, 'I don't think we'll bother decorating this year, George, there's little here to excite me.'

But if you wave the "Magic Wand of the Imagination" over those colours, you transform them: Off-white becomes Champagne Mist, Grey becomes Victorian Skies, Green becomes Swamp Fever and Pink becomes Flamingo Dreams. Et voila, you now have something to sell. Now we pull George from the power-drill display and show him the chart, 'George, I want Champagne Mist in the kitchen, Victorian Skies in the utility room, Swamp Fever in the bathroom, and Flamingo Dreams in the bedroom. Oh, George, we'll be together in Flamingo Dreams!'

Names add cache and mystique, colour, history, legend, association, power, humour, relevance, style, and panache.

You have just spent time in the previous module defining your end-user, so you've done some thinking on what language your audience speaks, and what words they use. You are about to find out how words evoke imagery and association in the minds of your end-users, and how these, in turn, elicit emotional states and responses.

A good name can add massive value to your brand. I personally love brand names that are a bit wry, such as the following fish bars: Your Plaice or Mine, Frying Nemo, The Codfather, and Lord of the Fries. I don't know if they do good chips but I know they've all got brilliant names.

---

'A good name is better than a girdle of gold.'
*French Proverb*

---

## What should a good name be?

A good name should be DURABLE.

When you've come up with what you feel could be a good name, all you need do is ask 'Is this name **D.U.R.A.B.L.E.**?' Here's how it works, a good name should be:

**Distinctive**

**Unique**

**Rememberable**

**Arbitrary**

**Broadcast-friendly**

**Likeable**

**Evocative**

Can your name be truthfully described by these seven key adjectives?

### Is your name Distinctive and Unique?

A brand name should be distinctive and unique. That is to say, it needs to be different. It needs to be different so it can stand out from other brands, and not be confused with anyone else. The more **distinctive** and **unique** your brand's name is, the better.

If there are twenty other Lord of the Fries in a given area, what value is that name giving you? Not much, mate. People may love it, but if it's not sufficiently Distinctive and Unique it's just RABLE (and no one wants that).

If your brand has the same name as—or a very similar name to—another pre-established brand, you risk marketplace confusion and legal action, which can negatively affect your ability to trade and grow.

If the confusion swings in your favour because you are mimicking, or "paying homage" to another brand—i.e. you are 'passing off' or deceiving people by harnessing the goodwill created by another pre-established brand—for example, if you call your brand 'Tarbucks Coffee' it could positively boost your ability to sell coffee, as people might ORATE you better, however, this is NOT good and most likely means your brand is infringing on the Intellectual Property and copyright of Starbucks, a pre-established brand.

If the brand you are mimicking is protected—a brand name is often protected by it simply being the first of its kind in its market—you risk legal action.

If the coincidental naming is just an unfortunate mistake, you still risk legal action from the pre-established brand with the same name. The burden of proof is on the other brand however it could have a strong case and because it was established before you, you will be asked why you didn't research the market sufficiently.

If you can hire the services of an IP Attorney I would recommend you do so, however, there are many search resources available and it's always worth researching as much as you possibly can before committing to—and releasing—your brand name, to ensure it is unique enough for your purposes.

> You want to avoid a name that is the same as—or very similar to—another one that already exists.
>
> When naming your brand, the two key pieces of advice are:
> –1). Be inventive! Come up with a distinctive and unique name
> –2). Research as much as you can to check it's not already being used.

Distinctive names are usually less likely to be already taken, less likely to be accidentally thought up by someone else, and more protected. The level of distinctiveness usually corresponds with the level of protection a name garners.

> The size and age of a brand name's 'meaningful connection'—between its goods or services and its audience—is also a big protective factor e.g. the brand name Pepsi has a large and long-established connection between its primary product and its end-user audience. The millions of people around the world who know of and use the product would make it easy for the brand to show it has existed as a brand name for a long time to a lot of people. Pepsi® is a registered brand name and is also part of a famous registered trade mark i.e. the distinctive red and blue logo.

In legal circles, the most distinctive name is an 'arbitrary' one i.e. a name with no obvious connection to the brand's trade or offering (see page 103).

Often, the less distinctive a name is, the less protection it garners.

In cases where the brand name describes its good or offering in a descriptive or semi-descriptive way—e.g. Passion Hair & Beauty—the critical legal factors will be its industry sector, the date it began trading, and its geographical location i.e. where the brand does its business.

Imagine Janine opens up her new hairdressing business called Passion Hair & Beauty on a high street somewhere in a town in England. Then imagine a brand called Passion Kebabs rocks up five doors down a few weeks later. Janine is incensed, 'how dare they?' she fumes, 'I'll make them change that name!'

But because Passion Kebabs is operating in a different industry sector, even though they are geographically close, Janine is unlikely to have a good legal case. However, if another hair and beauty brand sets up shop nearby, and is named, for example, Passion8 Hair & Beauty, then Janine could well have much stronger grounds to take legal action.

Like any legal action, it would depend on specific factors unique to the case, but Janine's key complaints would centre around marketplace confusion and the misappropriation of the goodwill that her brand name has built up over time.

The duration and strength of the connection between her trade, her brand name, and her trade audience of end-users, would be a key factor. If Janine had only been trading for a few weeks and hadn't registered her name (few hairdressers register their brand names), and hadn't got to know many clients, her case wouldn't be that strong.

But the bigger that connection grows—between brand, trade, and audience—the more power she has to challenge copycats.

And if her Passion Hair & Beauty were to become productised and in some meaningful way outgrow her geographical base (for example Aveda which started as a single salon in Minneapolis in 1978) Janine's brand could well achieve the power to sue any newcomer brands with the same name. And not only similar brand names in other towns but in other industry sectors too.

Everything counts in large amounts.

Most brand founders are keen to invent their own unique and distinctive names, for good solid reasons (personal and commercial) and most would like to avoid copying another brand, but it's worth considering the legal implications when coming up with your brand name.

It's easy to come up with a brilliant one only to find it's already in use by a more established business.*

Registering a brand name increases protection, however, in another twist, family surnames are usually not registrable as protected trademarks.†

Although, if your family name is distinctive—or is to operate in a field that makes it distinctive—that can help your chances of filing a successful trade name registration. Partnering up—e.g. as Jenson and Kingfisher—is also another way of creating a more distinctive name.

If a brand gets really big, it has the power to prevent *anyone*, in *any* industry from using the name. So no matter what you sell, don't name your brand McDonald's or even McRonald's.

> It's also worth remembering that the more distinctive and unique your brand name is, the better chance you have of registering it as a registered trademark, should you wish to add that extra level of credibility.

* The most likely instances of businesses and brands having the same name is when they are named after surnames e.g. Greebley & Sons. For the reasons mentioned above, it's very much in the interests of the creator of the business or brand to ensure no one else is using that name, and vital they do adequate due diligence.

However, because sole traders are not legally obligated to register their businesses, it can be hard to find all potential instances of the same, or similar, name to your own.

In the case of two small and proximate businesses called Greebley & Sons, the established brand could have a case to take legal action against the newcomer brand, however only if the newcomer was operating in the same industry.

If the new Greebley & Sons was in the same industry, for example plumbing and heating services, but operating in a different town, far far away from a small yet well-established Greebley & Sons, there would usually be no grounds for legal action.

That said, if the established Greebley & Sons grows beyond its one small independent local location—and starts servicing boilers the length of Britain—and can prove it has considerably extended its "reach" and has grown a meaningful trade-based connection with its audience, i.e. use and operations that precede the newcomer's use and operations—it usually has strong grounds for legal action against the newcomer.

And in such a case, the key concerns and complaints of the established brand would be that its end-users are quite likely to become confused and may easily assign the goodwill and reputation built up by the established brand to the newcomer brand.

The law is set up to protect against this and to prevent a business's copyright and Intellectual Property from being infringed or stolen by newcomer brands, within its zone of operation.

† There are exceptions to this e.g. Bang & Olufsen, WHSmiths and the US car brand Ford, but these brands are exceptional in many respects.

> A brand's recognised brand name or trademark can be—and often is—different from its official business name, e.g. FedEx is the brand name—or trademark—of the FedEx Corporation. Many brands are representative of limited or public companies in the UK but you needn't put Ltd in your brand's name, trademark, or URL.

Registered business names require approval from official governmental registries when they are being set up. However, it's worth remembering that a brand name—or 'trading name' or 'trade name'—is not necessarily registered anywhere, except through the brand's branding, marketing, and online presence. However, if the brand has actually registered its brand name or trademark—and achieved an '®' symbol—this will usually be listed and searchable.

What this all means is that finding a good distinctive handle gets harder every day, and so, you should be prepared to put in the necessary time to find a good one that is distinctive and unique.

'Username already taken' is a harsh sentence to read but it's better to find out as early as possible if your prospective name is already spoken for. If you come up with a great name and commission a load of stationery or signage, only to find out the name is already being used elsewhere, it can be embarrassing, painful, and expensive.

We live in the great "Age of the Internet" which is a blessing and a curse.

The curse is that once-highly-original Lord of the Fries fish bars are now showing up everywhere—the world's awash with Lord of the Friess. It's becoming ever harder to find a unique name. The blessing is that it is easier than ever before to see and check how unique your name is.

When I start a naming project, I usually view the origination of a new brand name as a two-part process i.e....

1). the finding,

and then...

2). the clearing—because quite often one finds a great name only to find it is being used elsewhere by another brand.

Sometimes, you find the name is being used in such a way that you can still use it. If it is available as a .com URL then that is usually a good sign and means it could be available, but that is only a clue.

Brandable channels with low bars to entry such as free email services and social media platforms, like Hotmail and X (formerly Twitter) usually make the job of finding a unique name, and using it, much harder because anyone can sign up at no cost and claim a name.

There are some great websites to help you such as ICANN WHOIS database and also namecheckr.com. The latter not only lists the main domain suffixes—e.g. .com, .co.uk—and whether they are available but also checks key social media handles.

Some websites allow you to check for registered trademarks and many will show you how to apply for domain names or register limited companies and brand names—i.e. trade names and trademarks and other forms of brand name protection.

I saw a cafe in East London called 'Tina, we salute you' which I thought was an amazing name, and probably quite unique, but it's always worth checking. Lord of the Fries is a strong name but if another one comes along, the name becomes weaker—in a land of many Lord of the Friess the lone Codfather is king.

In branding, being distinctive and unique is important and valuable, but with naming, it is vital.

## Is your name Rememberable?*

It doesn't matter how Distinctive and Unique your name is, if no one can remember it, it's wasted. However, if your brand name is distinctive and unique it is more likely to be rememberable I suppose.

You want your brand name to be "sticky" and stick in people's long-term memory, so they can recall you when they need to. When I tried to remember some brand names, the first to pop into my head were...

- A Touch Of Dutch (furniture shop in Surbiton)
- KFC
- Sony
- Nikon
- Nike
- Go Outdoors
- Pret
- Balenciaga (but I had to check the spelling)
- Carhartt
- Bodyshop.

These are all names I can recall, instantly, with ease, and pleasure,

* Yes, ok, Uncle Brian, maybe this should have been 'memorable', but that would have messed up my acronym, and besides, rememberable is a valid synonym.

giving them free advertising in the process. Seeing—and hearing—them in adverts, podcasts, social media, and product placement, probably helped but if you can't remember what a brand is called, then it becomes unavailable to you.

'George, what was that restaurant called we like? No, it's gone.'

If it is not available to you, you may find it very difficult to locate, use, or talk about that brand. People use and share that which is available to them. If your brand name is rememberable, it will last a long time.

## Is your name Arbitrary?

An arbitrary brand name is one with no obvious, inherent connection to the products or services it represents.

That is to say, it's the opposite of a generic name.

Apple is an arbitrary brand name. As is Porsche. As is Starbucks.*

Having an arbitrary name is advantageous for many reasons.

Not only are they distinctive and rememberable, they are also flexible and easier to protect.

Brands with arbitrary names are not bound to any one particular sector and can expand, if desired, into other sectors. For example, Adidas, Vaseline†, and Sprite are more 'arbitrary' than the fictitious alternatives of MegaSports, LubeyLube, and LimeyFizzPop—which are more descriptive in nature.

Arbitrary names are also less bound by language and can be adapted for international markets and become global success stories.

They are also more likely to receive strong legal protection because they are not generic or descriptive and so are naturally more creative and authored, and therefore protectable.

Because arbitrary names have no obvious pre-conceived connection to the brands, goods, and services they represent, they are seen as more creative names—more "authored".

* When it was first set up in 1971, *Starbucks* was originally called *Starbucks Coffee, Tea, and Spices*. It was set up in Seattle by three men: an English teacher named Jerry, a history teacher named Zev and a writer named Gordon. At one point in the process of finding their brand name, the writer, Gordon, was looking at an old mining map and saw a town named 'Starbo'. This reminded him of the character, in Melville's classic novel *Moby Dick*, called 'Starbuck'. Gordon took it to the others and they added an 's'. And thus they named their company 'Starbucks' and when future historians look back at any map depicting the early part of the 21st Century they will probably see many many Starbuckss.

† Vaseline is more inventive and distinctive sounding than the fictitious LubeyLube however interestingly, the brand name Vaseline was created by its manufacturer in a fairly prosaic fashion by sticking the German for 'water' i.e. 'wasser' with the Greek for olive oil i.e. 'elaion'.

## Is your name Broadcast-friendly?

The more broadcast-friendly your name is, the more it will be broadcast. That is to say the more people will enjoy using it, talking about it, and the further and wider it will travel. And you do want your brand name to travel. After all, a name is also called a handle, and so-called for good reason.

A good name should fall off the tongue.

And hit the ground running.

It should be robust and pass-on-able. You want people to be talking about your brand at the bus stop.

'You know, Jean, I love A Touch of Dutch ... yes, on the Ewell Road. Lovely garden furniture.'

And you want someone two seats down to be eavesdropping and pick up on your name and be able to go home and google it or talk about you.

Think about the sound. Aim for phonetic spellings where possible. If you must use a silent letter or a "cute" spelling make it so cute, distinct, and remarkable that anyone talking about you is compelled to remark on that feature.

The transportability of your brand name can be helped with SEO and other mechanisms, but do consider if, where, and how, your name could be misheard.

The term 'eggcorns' (coined by linguist Geoffrey Pullum in 2003) refers to a linguistic error, or slip of the ear, where a word or phrase is replaced by a similar-sounding one (eg: Chester drawers instead of Chest of drawers; Cold Slaw in place of Coleslaw). And while there's little you can do to second-guess every brain out there, it is worth thinking about where your name could be misheard.

Also, take special care if using special characters like ampersands (&)—those squiggly alternatives to the word 'and'—or cross signs ('+') also often used for this same purpose or any device that could easily be misconstrued or typed incorrectly into a search bar. Consider how the name affects your online presence, and how it would appear as a web address (URL). Many symbols and special characters are not allowed in your URL (Uniform Resource Locator) so do plenty of research.

Also, beware of using hyphens ('-') in your name and URL as this can add further confusion. If your name consists of two or more words, consider how they bunch together if placed in a URL, and ensure they don't inadvertently spell other words. Names like Welsh IT Services or Myar Sebum Analytics could be problematic.

The transportability of your name is key because your name is your most cost-effective digital asset, and we humans love nothing more than to talk about stuff. What I'm saying is: your name can make you or break you—and the broadcast-friendliness of your name will dictate how much traction and currency your brand accrues.

Also, think about how the name will transport visually when written or as part of a logo. Anything too long may give a designer problems when creating your branded materials or may give people writer's cramp when typing your name into a web search.

Transportability matters in how far your brand reaches, so the more broadcast-friendly you make it, the better. If it is broadcast-friendly your name will travel far and wide.

## Is your name Likeable and Evocative?

A good name should be Likeable and Evocative.

Words suggest imagery in the human mind.

When someone sees a word: images are conjured, feelings triggered and associations made.

Branding can be seen as a process—or an opportunity—of influencing people's perceptions. Just like Pavlov did with his dogs, you can do with your audience.

So say you've come up with a name. It's Distinctive, it's Unique, it's Rememberable, it's Authentic, and it's Broadcast-friendly, but does your audience Like what it Evokes? What images are conjured in the minds? And what feelings are evoked in people's hearts?

When we hear or see a name or any word, we create associations and mental imagery. Sometimes the imagery is weak and blurred (especially for those with aphantasia) and sometimes it is strong, decorative and detailed, but every time we hear a name, it triggers certain responses.

We humans have this part of our brain called the limbic system, which is responsible for generating emotional responses to the data our senses provide it. The limbic system is the "gatekeeper", or rather the "Designator of Emotions".

It's sort of like Ellis Island for sense data: the place through which everything must pass and be labelled accordingly. It's where names are given their status: 'From now on this name will be forever associated with pleasure, this name with pain, and that other one with guilt'. The amazing film Inside Out shows beautifully how this system works. It is a very powerful system.

Yes, actual images indeed have a little bit more, ahem, "limbic resonance" than words, and that's why Instagram is a little bit more popular than X (formerly Twitter)—but words still create powerful imagery. And what's more, words can be more widely embraced by people as they allow the reader or listener to create their very own 'self-made' imagery, which can make things more relatable, or rather, less unrelatable.

What emotions does your name generate in the brains of your audience?

You may have come up with the brand name Blue Dog, for example, and believe it to be highly Distinctive and Unique, Rememberable, Authentic, and Broadcast-friendly but how Likeable is it? And what does it Evoke?

This will depend on what you do and who you do it for.

If you create surfboards then brilliant. As we all know, there is nothing cooler than the image of a dog surfing blue water, or you may be a software company and that still works, provided 'Blue Dog' isn't the name of a virus.

However, if you're a doggie daycare business, then I would advise you that Blue Dog is <u>NOT</u> a good name, because, in this context, that name now suggests a sad and lonely dog. The limbic system will create bad feelings in your audience's brains on that one, 'George, I don't care how much discount they offered you, Buster is not staying at the Blue Dog Daycare Centre!'

Look at the luxury ice cream brand Häagen-Dazs—what imagery this name conjures up!—such indulgence, mystique, and elegance, so evocative to both my eyes and my ears.

What do those little dots mean? Why do you pronounce 'Dazs' as 'dars'? I see and hear this brand name and I feel an emotional change in my body. I want ice cream and now. I hear Häagen-Dazs and see slow-motion footage of playful fashion models in leather catsuits pillow-fighting in front of exploding flashbulbs.

But what does the name Häagen-Dazs actually mean?

Absolutely...

...nothing.

It was made up by the founders in 1961 and has no meaning at all. Plucked from thin air. It just looks and sounds great, and more importantly, evokes the right feeling, i.e. it's Sexy Ice Cream Time, which is perfectly suited to its audience, an audience that justifies hard-earned indulgence and is willing to spend that little bit extra, for the additional story of luxury and prestige this brand provides. Names add story. And story adds value.

If you just want a bit of low-end soft-scoop to keep the kids quiet, you'll probably go for a no-nonsense 'own brand' ice cream.* And it will probably be called 'ice cream'. Naming plays a big role in bringing greater value to named brands but these brands need to be "dressed authentically" and every aspect of their ACTivity needs to reflect the name and back story.

Most own brands are positioned and sold as 'commodities', a level down from 'experiences' and so use basic—and obvious—product descriptors. If they sell ice cream, they sell generic 'ice cream'. They don't mess about. However a named brand—with greater brand equity and latitude—could be more adventurous and could call ice cream something like Frozen Bliss.

'Frozen Bliss is not just an ice cream, George, it's an experience.'

Which of course, sets the stage for greater *Theatre!* and a potentially higher price point. I'm sure better ingredients and greater care and attention go into the production of named brands than into own brand products—but the greater value perceived by the discerning consumer is often based on much more than the product itself.

Good branding and good naming add value. 'Victorian Skies' is more valuable as a brand name than 'Grey' (also, in most cases, a simple descriptive name cannot be registered as a registered trade name).

The name of your brand can help influence its ultimate success, and so to come up with such a name is a great start to the whole process of building your brand.

Words have great power in naming and you can use them to paint vivid pictures that create imagery in the minds of your end-users.

* 'Own brands'—or 'white label' brands—are goods made especially for a retailer, for example *Sainsbury's*, and sold as *Sainsbury's* products. 'Own brands' are usually retailed at a lower price point than a 'named brand'.

Take for example Fat Willy's Surf Shack. What a great name. As cool today, as it was when it was founded in 1984 in the popular surfing town of Newquay, England. I didn't go to Cornwall myself until 2002 and by then I was already well into my twenties but all through my early childhood, I would see this brand's colourful logo—300 miles from Newquay—and I'd picture a wooden shack, surrounded by gnarly palm trees and wet-suited wave monkeys dowsing their peroxide blonde aqua-dreds in blue juice.

Even before they've met you, your end-users can be attracted by a DURABLE name and they can start to ORATE your brand, after seeing just a few careworn bumper stickers.

Likeability and Evocativeness matter. And what your name evokes will go a long way in determining likeability.

If your brand name evokes the right feelings, it will "get through the door" and earn a special place in the minds—and, more importantly, the hearts—of your audience.

Is your brand name likeable? Does it make you smile every time you say it?

Is it as good as 'Tina, we salute you'?

Does it fill your audience with joy every time they hear it?

If not, then you might want to search a bit harder for a name that is so awesome it lifts your spirits every day.

---

'To name oneself is the first act
of both the poet and the revolutionary.'
*Erica Jong*

---

## Can your name be DURABLER?

Yes, by adding the R of Regeneration.

Is your name Regenerative?

By 'regenerative' I mean, does your brand name lend itself to brand extension further down the line? Can it grow? Is it future-proof? Does it have the ability to accommodate possible changes in your brand's offerings? As mentioned before, this is where an arbitrary name can come in very handy.

Colonel Cockburn's Coffee for example is not as arbitrary as—and therefore less regenerative than—Colonel Cockburn's.

Virgin is a good example of a regenerative brand name—it lends itself to brand extension. The brand was easily able to extend into other sectors using its trusted name and identity. Virgin records. Virgin Atlantic. Virgincare.

Although perhaps the best example of brand extension is the easyJet brand. This brand just extended and extended.

easyJet. easyCar. easyBus. easyPizza. easyCoffee. easyHotel. easyOffice. easyProperty. easyGym. easyValue. easyCinema. easyMusic. easyEnergy. easyCruise. easyMobile. easyCoach, and many more.

The name and identity make the brand's offerings almost infinite.

## Surely my name can be anything I damn well want it to be?

Pretty much, as long as it is legal* and available† ... then yes it can be anything you damn well want it to be.

The idea is that through your brand you create a meaningful connection between your brand, its trade offering, and an audience. Look at the brand name Starbucks, it had no obvious connection to coffee when it was founded—however, it does now (and it certainly passes the DURABLE test).

Do get feedback from a variety of people whose opinions you trust, as I mentioned with Evocativeness, it pays to be mindful of what your brand name says about your brand.

* This will depend on where and how you intend to use your brand name but if the name is also your company name you will usually discover if it is legal, or not, during the registration of your company by the relevant legal bodies (in the UK, new companies must be registered with Companies House).

† i.e. not being used by anyone else in such a way that it would cause problems.

## So how do you find a good name?

There's a curtain and blinds shop in Maidenhead called Mainly Curtains & Blinds, a bar in New York called The Fat Black Pussycat. There's an alt-rock band called Unprovoked Moose Attack, a carbonated beverage called Pepsi, and a motorcycle brand called Harley-Davidson, you may have heard of it.

Great names are everywhere, but how do you find a great one for your brand?

You start looking. You start thinking. You start noting down ideas.

Don't go Van Gogh crazy looking for the perfect most awesome name, as it could evade you and keep you from the other important work—your name is after all, only part of your brand's story—but it *is* a big part, so search well, give yourself time, and factor in plenty of sleeps, changes of state, and try to encourage subtle shifts in perspective, so you can come at the challenge of finding a durable name from a wide variety of angles.

Such creative gold-digging can drive you mad but don't forget that the world wants to help you, the human mind is cool, and simplicity is often genius. Also, most people can usually think of the right answer pretty quick if they're sufficiently relaxed. But many also think it should be harder to find great names, so they may find a great one and dismiss it too quickly, thinking 'It can't be a good name because I thought of it and it came so easy'. So they insist on looking for other answers and make life difficult for themselves.

You can accelerate the process. If I'm up against a deadline and need to get creative fast, I like to create 'NameGrids' or 'NameBombs'.* For these, you'll need a brain, a piece of paper, a thesaurus (and a nice beverage).

For the NameGrid, the idea is to create several vertical columns of words across the page. Write out your keywords at the top. For example, imagine you've been asked to create a name for a parking system that requires the driver to pay a fee and then put a ticket in their window. So you write 'Pay' at the top of the first column, and then you write 'Show' at the top of the second column (you could add a third or fourth column but for now we won't). Under 'Pay' (in that column) you start listing synonyms (for 'Pay') such as 'Lend', 'Furnish', 'Provide', and

* Ok, Uncle Brian, sure, it's just a Spider Diagram. But 'NameBomb' is a better name, ok. It just is.

'Grant'. And under 'Show' (in that column) you start listing synonyms (for 'Show') such as 'Display', 'Divulge', 'Exhibit', and 'Herald'. If you're doing the NameBomb system you just take the keywords and put them in circles then arrange the attendant synonyms around the respective circles. So then you scan across the columns or word groups and play with relationships: 'Lend and Divulge', 'Furnish 'and Herald', 'Give and Show' and you may get disheartened and think about going out for a Cheekipop ... but then you see it: 'Pay and Display' and boom! it's business time.

Pay and Display huh, now there is a name that paid dividends. Why? Because it's brilliant. It's DURABLE, it's relevant and it rhymes. It even rhymes in the past tense: 'Have you paid and displayed?'

'Pay on foot' parking is a better system but it's a rubbish name. Where's the rhyme? The human mind loves rhymes, just like it loves puns or anything that suggests a special relationship or harmony between things. It's why we love music. We set up a question, or a discord, to then supply a tonic through some form of resolution, it just makes our brains happy, and gives us "closure".

## People love names that rhyme, every time

As we see with 'Pay and Display', names that rhyme stand the test of time.

A Touch of Dutch, anyone?

The brain just loves the poetic powerplay of a rhyme. Rhymes land and expand, they chime and climb, and they seal the deal.

Many brand names take advantage of rhymes because they charm without harm and they also help people remember the name. That's why rhymes are used so much in branding, adverts, and propaganda. They make the message tasty and sticky and people are more likely to trust something if it rhymes.

We find it in fashion with 'boob tubes', and 'crop tops', in the work of Charles Dickens with 'nitwit' and the Pickwick papers. We find it in just about every place where creative communicators choose to captivate their audiences.

It is no different in the case of brand names and trademarks. We just love 'em, trust 'em, and remember 'em all the more if they rhyme.

'George, I've just bought tickets from StubHub to go and watch Tears for Fears. I'll stop off at the Bread Ahead bakery and then pop to the 7-Eleven to get some Lean Cuisine, some Hubba Bubba, a Curly-wurly, some Reese's Pieces, and a Fruit Shoot. Maybe even a nice bottle of Rola Cola.'

Some people say 'rhymes are past their prime' (ironically), and that the idea of using rhyme is cheesy or old-fashioned, that rhymes can all-too-easily date or 'bracket' a brand if you're not careful. And they do have a point, you don't want to get stuck up "Cheese Avenue", I mean we're no longer in the 50s, or even the 80s, thank God. In his day, 'Ronald McDonald'—the lovable burger clown—was king of the world, but I notice he's adopted a slightly lower profile of late. But even so, as long as you are "staying relevant" to your audience, and "people are, like, responding"—rhyming is all good.

## Pun and games

It's important to be playful when coming up with your name.

It pays to play.

Being relaxed and playful can help you generate ideas, and think laterally.

Sometimes when you allow yourself to relax the usual laws of order, and meaning, you can merge things and create new stuff, and sometimes you hit gold and create a pun.

All naming—and indeed all language—is, in a sense, wordplay i.e. the playing with words. But the term 'wordplay' usually denotes a particularly 'clever' or 'cute' use of language, and puns are usually the chief product of this process. They often get bad press, because of their association with Christmas cracker jokes such as 'Santa doesn't smoke 'cos it's bad for his elf' etc. but good puns can work very well.

However, if a pun is good, relevant, and appropriate, it can help a brand stand out from the crowd and be remembered and shared easily for a very long time. There's a bespoke optician in London called Spex In The City, a rug company called Carpet Diem, a flooring specialist in Liss called On All Floors, and another in Dublin called Lino Richie.

## Does your name have a good in-built backstory?

Your brand name may be nonsensical at first glance or to the unlearned ear, but if it has a special reason why it has that name—such as an in-built back story that people can learn of and appreciate—it can make your brand all the richer and lead people to exclaim 'Ooh! that's interesting.'

If the reason why your brand got its name is relevant to your brand and yet obscure enough to make that not immediately obvious, it can create a powerful effect. Take Pepsi for example, we're all familiar with this world-famous product and yet did you know it was originally created by a frustrated doctor who had to become a pharmacist instead and took to formulating a health drink? He formulated this product to relieve indigestion and boost energy and took his brand name directly from the medical term for indigestion—dyspepsia—and the kola nuts used in his recipe to create the name Pepsi-Cola.

3M is a reference to its original company name Minnesota Mining and Manufacturing. IBM (International Business Machines) started out as ITR (International Recording Company) and went through various names. Bic was named after its co-founder Marcel Bich, but he dropped the 'h' to avoid likely mispronunciation. When Pierre Omidya was naming his company, he wanted the name EchoBay, but found the domain name was already taken, so instead, he just went for eBay.

And did you know that one of the biggest brand names on Earth is a typo? The founders—Larry Page and Sergey Brin—thought it was a cool name because it is also a mathematical term meaning a number so big it is expressed as a '1' followed by 100 zeros, however, the mathematical term is actually spelt 'googol'.

> Brand names should be DURABLE but that's not to say they can't come from prosaic places and do not be afraid to embrace the simple and obvious. When the Rocket Chemical Company was developing a rust-prevention spray in the 1950s, its inventor discovered the best way forward was through water displacement, and finally, he perfected the Water Displacement spray on the 40th attempt, so the company named the spray WD-40. And today, WD-40 is one of the most recognised brand names on Earth.

---

'You can't use up creativity.
The more you use, the more you have.'
*Maya Angelou*

---

> Don't throw anything away. During the process of generating name ideas you'll probably come up with loads of stuff you deem 'not quite good enough' ... but you're sure to discover volumes of interesting material. Material which might lend itself to other uses down the road (e.g. Content creation).

## Consider a 'cut-and-shut'

Cutting up parts of two different words and fusing them together can create interesting new words. Such a word is called a 'portmanteau' and the portmanteau can be very helpful to the brand creator. This linguistic naming device helps you to create a new word while also including an oblique yet relevant reference to your reason-for-being. For example, the brand name LEGO is a portmanteau of the two Danish words 'leg' and 'godt', which mean 'play well'. The delivery brand FedEx is a portmanteau of 'Federal Express'* The delivery brand YODEL is a portmanteau of 'YOUR' and 'DELIVERY'—and 'YOUR DELIVERY' is also its primary strapline.

Playing with prefixes and suffixes is a very useful exercise in coming up with new names. One can use words from other languages and have some fun, and with access to the internet making information more available, the process "just got easier". Choose creative combinations and stay ahead of the competition. You can plunder all sorts of places for words to cut-and-shut, other languages, other words, verbs, nouns, German, Greek, Spanish, and Latin.

The rye-based snack brand Ryvita was named by cutting and shutting 'rye' and 'vita'—'vita' is Latin for 'life'. Cutting and shutting 'pin' and 'interest' gives you Pinterest, 'Britain' and 'exit' gives you Brexit, and of course 'shark' and 'tornado' gives us Sharknado.

* Federal Express was the original brand name, before it was cut-and-shut to make FedEx.

## Think about the sound it makes

We humans communicate via sounds—and we did so a long time before someone started writing them down into written codes and alphabets. It's believed humanity has created around 7000 spoken languages in total—which were of course created from using sounds. And it's also believed humans can make around 500 distinct sounds with their mouths, all told.

These sounds are known as phonemes and are—in language terms—the smallest packet of sounded information available. All languages are created by sequencing these phonemes together either as individuals or blends. The word 'four' has three phonemes blended together: the 'f', the 'ou', and the 'r'.

Let's check out some of these phonemes and see how they feature in some famous brand names...

*Plosives are explosive.*

The most impactful phonemes are the plosives. These are caused by creating a barrier through which no air can pass, then releasing it all in one go—the sound-making equivalent of a finger flick. The plosive sounds are 'P', 'B', 'G' ('guh'), 'D' ('duh'), 'K', and 'T'—and many brand names use these plosive phonemes because they create very satisfying and powerful sounds that get attention.

*'B' is boombastic*

Boh! The bassy 'B' is a beloved beginning to many a brilliant brand name. Examples include: Budweiser, Becks, Breitling, BT, Brother, Bang & Olufsen, Ben & Jerrys (Double ampersand alert), Boots, Benetton, BOSS, Bally, Balenciaga, Bandai, Barclays, Birkenstock, Bacardi, Band-Aid, British Airways, Burberry and Burger King and the never not brilliant Bosch which—thanks to ballsy Britons— is now part of everyday speech, 'so he's passing one defender, then he passes another, and then he puts it away. Top corner. Bosch!'

*Pop it with a 'P'*

The 'Pee' sound possesses power and passion and punches people in the ears—examples include: Pepsi, Pathé, Panini, Panavision, Panasonic,

P&O (Ampersand!), Porsche, Polydor, Prudential, Polaroid, Paiste, Peugeot, and Pedigree Chum.

*Blend with a 'Bl'*
Sounds like the phoneme-blending 'Bl' in 'blue' and Bloomingdales are plosives, as well as the pleasant 'Pl' found in plentiful examples such as in Plasticine, Playstation and Planet Hollywood.

*Go go go with a gorgeous 'G'*
The 'Guh' sound gives as good as it gets and goes gangbusters in brand names such as: Google, Guinness, Gap, Gulfstream, Guardian, Goop, Guess, Gordon's, and Goodmans.

*Dazzle with a 'D'*
'Dee' is determined. It's decent, dynamic, and dare I say, dope. It's dependable, dazzling, delicious, and deft, and demands—and deserves—deference. Examples include: Delta, Dove, Dell, Diesel, Disney, Dr Pepper, and Dunkin Donuts.

*Kick it with a 'K'*
The 'K' sound—also known by linguists as the 'voiceless velar stop'—is made by blocking airflow from the throat with the back of your tongue. 'K' is thought to be a very arousing and provocative sound with a lot of "cut-through". Comedians—people very sensitive to how certain sounds can excite audience reactions—often say 'K' is the king of our communicative sounds. It kicks off many famous brand names such as Kellogg's, KitKat, Carex, and Coca-Cola.

(An effective phoneme doesn't have to appear at the front of a word, the 'K' sound still kicks ass in Spanx and Oxfam.)

*Dentalise that plosive!*
Some plosives are dentalised plosives, which means they are created by placing the tongue against the teeth to make the sound, which is probably why the word 'teeth' is dental. The 'T' sound is a dentalised plosive and it has a very satisfying percussive 'hi-hat' quality that cuts through the air with the same acoustic signature as a fly being fried in an Insect-o-cutor. 'T' is a popular start to many brand names, such as Tinder, Toyota, TATA, Tesla, Toshiba, Texaco, TED, Timberland,

Target, Top Gear, Twix, Tupperware, Ticketmaster, TGI Fridays, Taco Bell, TAG, TIME, Timex, Tetrapak, Toblerone and Topshop.

*When you don't want the fireworks of a plosive, humanise with a 'Huh'.* 'P's and 'B's may pop and blast you, 'K's and 'T's may catch attention but the 'H' comes from the heart. The 'H' sound—a.k.a. the 'voiceless glottal fricative'—is sometimes called the aspirate.

The effort a person needs to make to produce a 'Huh!' often results in more vibration around the chest than in 'P', 'B', 'T', and 'K' words. I'm not sure how significant this is but it's interesting that words like 'Home', 'Heart', and 'Human' feature strong 'H's, and do so across various languages. 'Home' is 'Hom' in Hindi, 'Zuhause' in German, 'Huis' in Dutch, 'Hejmo' in Esperanto and 'Heim' in Icelandic. 'Heart' is 'Hjerte' in Danish, 'Herz' in German, and 'Hart' in Dutch. Brands that feature 'H' include: Honda, HP Inc, Hyundai, and The Home Depot.

*Lo! How we all like an 'L'*

Is there any more lovely a letter? I've always had affection for the letter 'L'. I'm called 'Luke' and I love that instant sense of expertise and authority I get when driving behind a Learner driver but beyond my little world there is still something luminous about the 'L' and the sound it makes.

I love 'Liberation', 'Lips', 'Light', and 'Love'. I love the way it's used in French, Spanish, and Italian as L' and La and Le and Les. It is a sensual sound, the sound of L'amour, and as The Beatles once sang 'Love is all you need.' Look at—and listen for—L'Oreal, LEGO, Louis Vuitton, Lexus, and Lipton, Lee, and Lacoste, Land Rover, Lufthansa. Lush.

*Raa with an 'R!'*

If you really want to rip it up, think about using an 'R' sound—a.k.a. the 'rhotic consonant'. This racey letter is sometimes referred to as the 'littera canina' or canine letter, because it can sound like the snarl of a dog, at least that's what the nurse in Romeo and Juliet said.

Maybe that's why it's so racey and rousing, but regardless of 'R's relative growl, it is ripe for use and rightly takes its place in the ritzy realm of real brand name royalty—'R' features in the names Remington, Ryvita, Ribena, Ralph Lauren, Reebok, Ray-Ban and Red Bull.

*Make it mellow and mouth-watering with an 'M'*

Except for a few languages, the 'M' sound is pretty much universal among humans and is usually the first sound a human will make, asking for milk from its 'Mama', 'Om', 'Mom' or 'Bungkam', or similar.

'M' is known as a 'bilabial nasal sound', meaning this sound needs the nose and both lips, which makes it hard for a ventriloquist with a cold to say McDonald's, Microsoft, Macy's, Majestic, Michelin, Mitsubishi, Mazda, M&S (Ampersand!), Mastercard, Amazon or Mercedes-Benz. Also, it features in 'My' which is often a good and empathetic word in a brand name, suggesting something your end-user can make their own.

*Make it any sound you like!*

Within reason. As long as your brand name is DURABLE and doesn't sound like any other brand name, you can make it any sound you like. These naming ideas are just that, ideas—to help you think about what your name could be.

The beautiful thing about brand names is they can be anything you like, provided they are legal, and the DURABLER they are, the better. If you're using English you can use whichever of the 26 letters of the alphabet works best. But always appreciate the sound of names. Names are just words, and words are sounds, and in naming, the sound of words is important, as any comedian or songwriter will tell you. Songwriters have long seen the value of using and arranging plosives and 'k's and rhotics and nasalised sounds to create the iconic soundbites that come to build the soundtracks of history. Listen to just about any hit song over the last eighty years.

Sounds sell.

I apologise to all the other letters I've overlooked.

'V' sound, you're victorious in Volkswagen, Visa, Volvo, Valentino, Volvic, Verizon, Vans, Versace, and Vivienne Westwood.

'J' sound, you're jubilant in Jeep, Jaffa Cakes, Jaguar, and John Lewis (and Gillette).

'S' sound, we salute you. You're seeing to success in Samsung,

Samsonite, Sainsbury's, Starbucks, SONY, Siemens, STIHL, Sigma and Stella Artois.

And wait, what? I overlooked 'W'? ... you're doing worthy work in Wacom, Walmart, Warehouse, Wisdom, Western Union, Wilkinson, Wedgwood and Wonderbra. (And the brand name Huawei starts with a 'wuh' sound.)

## Does your name travel well?

We have just covered some thoughts on what sounds your name could use, but remember that not all sounds are used in all languages. 'P' doesn't really feature in Arabic and 'L' and 'R' sounds don't feature in many Southeast Asian languages, and if they do—such as with Thai—they are usually interchangeable. So whatever name you choose, consider how it will travel overseas and whether it could mean something rude in another language.

As you scale up your operations and reach wider audiences it's very possible you could be looking to operate in other countries, but if your brand name means something undesirable or hilariously unsuitable in another country—it doesn't matter how many modifications and accommodations you make because—your name may make it impossible to set up shop there.

Mazda launched a new minivan called Laputa, however in Spanish slang 'la puta' means 'the whore'. And apparently, Nokia had a similar naming problem with its Lumia smartphone, as 'lumia' is a Spanish slang term for prostitute. The first rule of naming: check the word isn't Spanish for prostitute.

When Ford released its first 'subcompact' car—the Ford Pinto in 1971—it was targeted at the kind of petrolhead who would be impressed with the two-litre engine and 38 cubic feet of cargo space. However to Brazilians, the word 'pinto' means 'tiny male genitals' which isn't the best phrase to market a high-performance automobile with.

Of course, there are also brands from other countries that would probably require renaming if they ever tried coming to the UK—such as the Finnish potato chip Megapussi and the Ghanaian hotly-spiced pepper sauce Shito.

There are however, many well-known brands that were founded

overseas yet still enjoy global reach—and operate very successfully across multiple countries—which have names that when translated into English actually reveal a pleasant surprise. For example, Mitsubishi is Japanese for 'three diamonds', which is reflected in the brand's logo.

## Think about rhythm and alliteration

Another good way to create a DURABLE name is to use rhythm. A name with rhythm gets remembered and shared. One reason why poems often have such widespread appeal is because the poet builds rhythm into her words. Rhythm can be appreciated by the reader no matter how much they agree with the content.

Rhythm relates to the 'song' that a sequence of words creates, and is separate to the 'meaning' the words convey. But when you combine rhythm with meaning the effect is explosive. It is the reason why folk songs passed through generations thousands of years before the age of literacy and the invention of printing. Sure, a songwriter—or poet—usually has more words with which to 'build in' rhythm but no matter how long your name is, it's always good to consider how it feels in the mouth and the ear.

Because your name will most likely be limited to a modest handful of characters, one good way to add rhythm to your name is to think about alliteration. Alliteration is the process of using words that feature the same letters, for example, Rolls-Royce, Dunkin' Donuts, Bed Bath & Beyond (Ampersand!), Krispy Kreme, 'Road Island Red', and although not a brand name "Credit Crunch" caught the public imagination. One of the most economical yet rhythmic brand names is Coca-Cola. That's a mini jazz show of a name.

---

'You campaign in poetry,
you govern in prose.'
*Mario Cuomo*

---

## Maybe even use your own name

Ever heard of Klaus Märtens? He was a doctor in the German army during the 2nd World War. While on leave in 1945, he injured his ankle skiing in the Bavarian Alps, and wouldn't you know, he found that standard-issue army boots were not great for his injured foot. So he made something that was. And he did it so well, he created a product that others wanted too. It's now one of the most well-known footwear brands in the world, named after the creator himself, Doc Martens.

If you are a personal brand—such as a sales trainer, hypnotherapist, hairdresser, or photographer—then using your own name may be the preferred route for you.

And it's a reasonable, effective, and authentic route, to naming your brand, but remember what we said about the importance of being arbitrary. Many brands feature the founder's name in front of a trade or service descriptor such as Juan Beauchamp Hairdressing or juanbeauchampphotography.com.

Which (as we saw with Colonel Cockburn's Coffee) could limit you down the line.

The obvious solution (to becoming more DURABLE) is to drop the trade or service descriptor—or relegate it to your strapline—and simply go with Juan Beauchamp, which can help on many levels and even add an extra layer of panache and mystique.

However, while this would make your name more arbitrary and ipso facto, more protectable, it would also, rather paradoxically, open you up to greater competition, as there could exist other Juan Beauchamps out there, decreasing the chance of you scoring a good domain name. And could also compromise company registration and trade name and trademark registration.

> We live in a world where multiple Juan Beauchamps can peacefully coexist and serve their respective audiences, but there cannot be two juanbeauchamp.coms, so tread carefully.

## One day you may merge

The history of multinational business is peppered with the merging of companies and who knows, one day your brand could merge with another. Obviously, it's not really something you should factor into your naming process—the merging of brand names is usually one of those bridges you should cross only when you come to it—but it's still helpful to look at how some brands have handled the job.

Some brands are now so fused in the minds of their audiences, that it is almost unimaginable to think of a time when the component names once led separate lives.

In 1891, Massey Manufacturing merged with A. Harris, Son & Co (Ampersand!) to become Massey-Harris and in 1953 Massey-Harris merged with the Ferguson Company to become Massey-Harris-Ferguson. It appears they simply stuck their names together, not exactly rocket science, but a bit of a mouthful with the triple-barrelled name. However, five years later they saw sense and in 1958 it was shortened to become the well-known agricultural machinery brand Massey Ferguson, famous for the tractors we know and love today. Proof that brands can merge and come out the other side with a DURABLE name.

Here are a few more...
- Time Warner
- ExxonMobil
- GlaxoSmithKline (GSK)
- Kraft Heinz
- PriceWaterhouseCoopers (PWC)

---

'When people use your brand name as a verb,
that is remarkable.'
*Meg Whitman*

---

## The verb test

The ultimate accolade of a brand name is for it to become part of everyday language as a verb.

'Can you hoover your room?' 'Could you xerox that document?'

'Will someone please taser that buffoon?' 'Oh just google it!'

Imagine someone using your brand name to describe the offering you provide: 'Ok, so we need this

[______________________________]ed immediately, like right now!'

## What do you do when you've found your name?

So, when you've found a DURABLE name, you do three things:

- you protect it
- you champion it
- you honour it.

### How do you protect a brand name?

This is a staged process. Firstly you start by being sufficiently satisfied that your name is Unique and Distinctive enough—for your uses—then you take steps using escalating levels of protection. Begin by shoring up the online platforms like web domains and social media accounts and then you can register for trade names and trademarks if necessary.

It's like insurance, in that the level of protection you choose will suit your attitude to risk and how you wish to use your budget. Do your due diligence though and check that your brand name is unique, if you take a name someone is already using you are infringing on their copyright and ignorance is no defence. Defensive legal action can be expensive and it's not a great use of budget if the problem was avoidable and largely created by your own short-sightedness. Plus, it can be embarrassing to strut your new brand name about, only for someone to point out there's another brand of that name. It is important you start using your brand name as soon as possible, to establish a meaningful connection between your brand and your audience. The size and age of that connection correspond to how protected your name becomes. The bigger your audience and the longer you connect with that audience, the better.

If you are totally satisfied you have chosen a unique and distinctive—and preferably 'arbitrary'—name and you have established a meaningful connection between your brand and an audience, then it's a good idea to register your name as a registered trade name. Registered trade names have a high level of protection. Having a registered trade name also clears the way for developing your brand identity, as you can proceed in the process knowing you're unlikely to face infringement problems down the road, and you'll be more likely to register your logo as a registered trademark.

To register your brand name as a registered trade name so it can carry the ® symbol—you will need to contact the relevant agent or authority in your territory. In the UK, such an application can be made through the HMRC website (www.gov.uk). This will tell you what you can and can't register as a trade name.

> Go through the correct channels when registering your trade name. Just because you secured a domain name or got your company registered as an incorporated or limited company does not make your name a registered trade name.

## How do you champion a brand name?

Simple: be proud of it. It arrived at your doorstep and you earnestly checked it had no rightful owner so you took it in and gave it a loving home. So now, be damn proud of it. Sure, there'll be haters. No matter how good a name you came up with, there will always be someone who says 'I don't like your name, it reminds me of pants'.

You can't please everyone.

## How do you honour a brand name?

Go the distance with it, be there for it. You've come up with a great name but after a time it loses its sparkle because familiarity breeds contempt. Unless you have a very good reason, do resist the temptation to change your brand name. You wouldn't change your child's name, would you? 'Alan, we've done some focus group work and we've decided to change your name to *Alfonso*, it has so much more je ne sais quoi.'

You are building up a solid foundation for your brand: you now have a why that reminds you why you do what you do; you have an ethos that reminds you how you do it; an end-user profile that shows you who you do it for, and you now have a DURABLE name—and maybe even a DURABLER one.

But make sure it does endure. If you have a domain name registered, ensure that it doesn't expire. Or someone could steal your name!

**Write and check your name by downloading the worksheet at: giveyourselfabrand.com/findyourname**

## STEP 5

# Give your brand a line

What one **line** beautifully sums your brand up?

## What is a line and why do you need one?

Your brand's line is a message in a bottle, sent out to the world to impart and convey why it exists.

It is your definitive primary audience-orientated statement and should attract, intrigue, educate, and connect.

Everyone has a line these days. Bakers, casinos, cycle shops, fictional characters. Even James Bond 007 has a strapline: 'Licence to kill.'*

A good line is a mini advert that can guide and steer all your brand's future adverts. A good line can do a lot of work in both informing, instructing, and reminding, your end-users why you are relevant to them. A line can instruct.

Memorable instructions are valuable. When I get a tea break I usually want a cup of tea, a walk, and something to eat—I could reach for a packet of crisps, a biscuit, or some carrot sticks ... but you know what I usually eat nine times out of ten? A KitKat. And I usually buy it from Tesco.

(The geographic location of your goods and services is a significant factor when it comes to driving footfall and sales but people do not always just choose the closest, we will happily walk past one general store to reach another we much prefer and trust i.e. ORATE more.)

But back to lines—here are a few examples of some great brand lines that sum up the brands they are selling so effectively in so few words:

'Every little helps' (Tesco).

'Because you're worth it' (L'Oreal).

'Never knowingly undersold' (John Lewis).

'be together not the same' (android).

'The best a man can get' (Gillette).

'Save Money. Live Better' (Walmart).

'Love it or hate it' (Marmite).

'The Power of Dreams' (HONDA).

'Vorsprung durch Technik' (Audi, it means 'Progress through Technology').

* Always made me wonder what the other agents' straplines were, maybe 009 'Licence to maim' or 004 'no job too small'.

Producing such a line requires much effort, and thought, but take comfort in the fact that by now you have worked out why your brand exists, you have articulated and defined its ethos, and values, who it serves, and what it is to be named.

And so you are now very well placed to write a meaningful line that encapsulates and communicates all this to your brand's audience. It's just a question of coming up with some options and working them out a bit, to find the right message and 'voice'—of which more later.

All communication requires a degree of assumption and is dependent on the relationship between the communicator and the audience. When you're having a conversation you can adapt, react, and change the information to suit the flow. But when you're writing a timeless strapline you've just got to create something that will go the distance and remain meaningful to its audience for a long time.

The more you know your audience, the better you can talk to them and write for them. And the more esoteric your buzzwords can be. However, the best straplines manage to deliver a great message while also maintaining broad accessibility and appeal.

Words have great power but only when you choose the right ones. You can't just say words and expect great power—believe me, I've tried.

So choose the best sequence of words because a great line is a valuable asset for any brand.

There is a distinction between your brand's line and its ethos. Your brand's ethos is not necessarily designed to be communicated overtly to your audience, whereas your line is designed to be overtly communicated to your audience.

It's a good idea to read through your ethos when writing your brand's primary line and you may even wish to use your ethos, or part of it, as the line itself, but whatever sentence you choose, choose it well.

You may choose to base your line on your brand's primary value offering but be aware this has pros and cons. It can help build relevance but can also limit you going forward. For example, L'Oreal's line 'Because You're Worth It' does not point to specific products, whereas 'Have A Break, Have A KitKat' does.

A brand like L'Oreal can have other slogans for specific product lines*, of course, and many 'parent brands' do house a stable of household brands with their portfolios. For example, the primary line for Kellogg's

* Here 'lines' means 'range'; as in 'product range'. Note the distinction.

is 'Let's make today great' but its product Kellogg's Frosties is known for the strapline 'They're GR-R-R-reat!'

So take care if aligning your primary line with your current value proposition as that could limit opportunities for future brand extension. And what if your primary value proposition changes? Sure, you could change your line, but consistency is king with branding, so think long-term.

A line is not always necessary. Sometimes the primary statement a brand wishes to communicate is already sufficiently communicated in its name (webuyanycar.com) but in most cases, the line is most necessary. This valuable and hard-working piece of copy serves to intrigue, inform, and inspire your audience, building trust and staying fresh over long periods.

The ultimate achievement for a brand's line is to become part of everyday language. Like Ronseal's famous line 'Does exactly what it says on the tin'.

In the previous section, while creating your name, we looked at how words evoke imagery and associations in the imaginations of the reader, and how this influences a reader's emotions and perceptions. It is, of course, the same story with your line, so having a good idea of your brand's audience will help you choose the right words that trigger the right images, associations, and emotional responses.

The most important thing about your brand's line is what it means to its audience and how it makes its readers feel. What do you want your audience to feel? What can you say to make it feel this way? Which words do you feel will say it in one go? Can you word it differently? Does the line use pronouns? From whose point of view is the line coming from? The brand's or the audience's?

Is it a first-person declaration? 'i'm lovin' it' (McDonald's).

Is it a suggestion? 'Have a break, Have a KitKat' (KitKat).

Is it a piece of advice? 'Buy local, buy safe' (Academy Home).

Is it a question? 'Maybe she's born with it, maybe it's Maybelline?' (Maybelline).

Is it a stern and specific command? 'Obey Your Thirst' (Sprite).

Is it a vague and open-ended command? 'Just Do It' (Nike).

Is it a bold claim? 'The Happiest Place on Earth' (Disneyland).

Is it a modest reference to the brand's provenance? 'ROMA' (Fendi).

Most importantly, does it ring true with the brand, will it empower your brand, will the audience get it and will they respond positively?

## Should a brand's line be DURABLE too?

We looked at DURABLE names earlier—and yes, your line should also follow an acronym very similar to this, but, there's a caveat. We need to lose the 'A'.

A line should be Distinctive, Unique, Rememberable, Broadcast-friendly, Likeable, and Evocative ... definitely.

But it should not be Arbitrary.

In fact, it should be the opposite. That is to say it should be relevant to how your brand delivers value. So, let's drop the 'A'.

'What?' frowns Brian, rolling his eyes, 'DURBLE'?

Yes, the more DURBLE your line is, the more chance it has of gaining traction with your audiences and the more value it will provide your brand.

## And can it also be DURBLER?

We looked at adding the 'R' of Regeneration to your name, but this is less important with a brand's line. You can consider making your line regenerative but it's less of an issue. Of course, one additional virtue a line should have—beyond the six that make up DURBLE—is the virtue of Relevance. A name needn't be relevant—as it simply serves as a "handle"—but, as we will see in a moment, a line's job is to "sell the dream" and so it should be relevant to your brand. So yes, a line can be DURBLER, only the 'R' stands for 'Relevant'. A brand name can, and should, be arbitrary, whereas a strapline should be relevant and express the essence of what you do and why you exist.

---

'Raise your words, not your voice.
It is rain that grows flowers, not thunder.'
*Rumi, 13th Century Sufi mystic*

---

## So how do you find a good line?

A line requires you to put together a sequence of words in a meaningful way and considering there are so many words to choose from—no matter what language you're using—this can often be difficult work. The following considerations and pointers should help you come up with a line that does your brand justice.

### Sell the dream!

This doesn't necessarily mean you have to sell the benefits in an overt or obvious way but rather your line should position your brand in such a way that your audience is compelled to come with you.

This is where you can maybe reflect some of your brand ethos.

When people read your line, you want them to instantly feel what it is your brand stands for and what it can do for them. This will depend on your brand, its offerings, and what your audience wants.

Brands vary in their ACTivity so naturally their styles and audiences are all different, and their lines will differ, but foremost, you want your audience to read your line and be educated, reminded, and compelled to come closer, feel inspired, assured, and desirous to engage further.

A brand's line can sell the dream via a no-nonsense descriptive nod towards its primary offering or it can be a wee bit more abstract or arbitrary, there are no exact rules—apart from the obvious i.e. it shouldn't copy another brand's line and it shouldn't feature obscene, racist or misogynistic language.

The more abstract a line is, usually the more distinctive and unique it becomes, which can help your brand stand out more, however, you have to exercise caution that the line is not too abstract. You may want the line to work in isolation from your identity i.e. your logo—or 'trademark'—for example, if your brand's line goes viral and segues into everyday speech to become a popular catch-phrase, like 'Because you're worth it' (L'Oréal). Large and well-established brands such as L'Oréal may have larger marketing budgets than you, but as long as you are brilliant, creative, and relevant, have a good online presence, and capture people's imaginations, there's no reason why your line can't catch fire and go viral.

Abstract lines still tend to sell the benefit in some way—even if the benefit may appear surreal, vague, or not immediately obvious. Lines such as: 'Taste the rainbow' (Skittles), 'Ideas for Life' (Panasonic), and 'Think Different' (Apple, 1997-2002). These abstract lines may appear strange at first glance, but they are very well-considered statements perfectly suited to position the brand where it needs to be positioned i.e. in the hearts and minds of the end-user and target demographics.

Some brands sell the dream using metaphor, as this can paint a distinctive picture in people's minds while usefully describing the benefits in a more emotive way. 'Sell the sizzle, not the sausage!' as they say. Some brand straplines that make good use of metaphor include: 'Unlock the world's larder' (Merchant Gourmet), 'Central heating for kids' (Ready Brek, 1980s), and 'Put a tiger in your tank' (Esso, 1964).

Some brands sell the dream more directly, by simply saying what the brand does or what it is—for example: 'Helpful Banking' (NatWest), 'Probably the Best Beer in the World' (Carlsberg), and 'The Ultimate Driving Machine' (BMW).

## Economy helps, so think about curtness

People haven't got all day to be reading your brand's primary line, so keep it short, keep it curt. It is called a 'line' after all, not a 'paragraph'.

You don't have to be too short—the conveyance of a good message is more important than the particular word count, for example, two words are not necessarily better than seven—but economy is valuable.

Brevity is, after all, the soul of wit.

Always see if you can rewrite your line to be shorter. If you can say twelve words instead of eight, say eight. Iteration and distillation are valuable processes in writing. Good writing is rewriting, so work your lines, and then work them again.

Some examples of economical lines include 'Eat Fresh' (Subway), 'INNOVATION' (3M), and 'THINK BIG' (IMAX).

---

'The secret of being boring is to say everything.'
*Voltaire*

---

## Curtness needs context

You only have to look at action films to see the value of curtness when it comes to delivering a good line. They're called one-liners for a reason.

And when you're walking away from an explosion, the less you say, the cooler you look. You must never point at the explosion and say 'Wow, look at that. I wonder how hot it is'. It's the same if you come face-to-face with a hostile alien, do you drone on about how it is missing a momentous opportunity to converse with a fellow being of the universe?—no, you punch it in the face, and say 'Welcome to Earth' (Captain Steven Hiller, Independence Day), and when your cocaine-financed dream house is being invaded by gun-toting henchmen, you don't start reading aloud excerpts from War and Peace, you introduce everyone to your biggest manageable machine gun with the phrase 'Say hello to my little friend.' (Tony Montana, Scarface).

Curtness in communication is appreciated—simplicity is value and word choice is key. The strength of these lines lies in their curtness, however, as good as these lines are, they only work because they operate within the contextualising framework of the film—within the unfolding story and all the drama that supports that story. If one of these one-liners were to be heard in isolation by someone outside of the film, in real life—with nothing to contextualise it—it would most probably be meaningless or confusing. I used to hear my friends at school say things like 'You're only supposed to blow the bloody doors off' and they'd fall about laughing, and I'd think 'What doors?' because I had not seen The Italian Job at that point. I remember a dim guy a few years above us at school called John pushing me and some friends around in a classroom declaring 'I'm the Daddy now! I'm the Daddy now!' And I remember us all just looking at each other in complete bewilderment because we were unaware he was quoting a line from the film Scum.

Consider your audience, John.

If you have created a big presence in your market and have a large audience aware of what your brand is all about, and how it rolls, you can use artistic licence and use private 'in jokes' to build rapport. After all, we humans are intelligent and sophisticated communicators who bore quickly and do not like being patronised. So creative uses of language can add value. However, if your line is too oblique or 'too clever' for your main audience you could be shooting yourself in the foot. Always try to put yourself in the shoes of prospective end-users, cater to the portions of your audience with less knowledge of your history and offerings, and sway your communications in their favour. Beyond your line, with your wider Content creation, PR, and marketing you can aim certain messages towards certain audiences, but with your line—which should remain as universally accessible as possible—always consider the context in which it is being read.

The two key purposes of a brand's primary line are to position the brand and sell the benefits. However, it can of course be used to sell the features of the brand's specific offerings.

Some brands employ interesting and creative use of language, whereas others simply use a no-nonsense list, for example, many hotels choose something like 'HOTEL RESTAURANT SPA'—and many construction companies opt for a services-focused line, such as 'Full project management' or 'All aspects of building.'

If you are a fashion label or a well-established department store you might want to consider something a bit more oblique and exotic. The top-level primary line of the M&S brand is simply 'EST. 1884' and the strapline of the brand Givenchy is simply 'PARIS'. If your brand enjoys a well-established presence, it can be appropriate to employ such brevity. Obliqueness can be valuable in terms of positioning but if you're a start-up lawn care company the strapline 'EST. 2018' might not be such a good choice.

## Should your primary line be a rhyme?

As with names, so it is with lines: rhymes can be valuable. A rhyming line can stand the test of time—because people are more likely to remember it and trust it. It's why rhymes are used in public messaging from advertising to wartime propaganda.

We genuinely believe 'Beanz meanz heinz' and that 'loose lips sink ships' and if I see the phrase 'Wash n' squash' I'm hungry to recycle.

I have full faith in the dietary advice that a 'Mars a day helps you work, rest and play', and if I notice my carpet looks a bit ropey I just 'Shake 'n vac' and put the freshness back'.

Other examples of rhyming straplines include: 'The appliance of science' (Zanussi, 1981), and 'Don't just book it, Thomas Cook it' (Thomas Cook, 1984). These lines are no longer used by the brands but I found them easy to recall. Me, the man with a terrible memory.

A rhyming line does tend to make the brand warmer and friendlier but that may not be the right 'voice' for your brand, for example, if you are a slick fashion label or a dignified undertaker—a rhyming strapline might not scan so well. But if you feel a rhyme would be a good fit for your brand, do it, because lines that rhyme are more likely to be loved, shared, and remembered. If you create a rhyming line, and keep it for the long haul, you're unstoppable, a thought best expressed by the primary line of Pringles: 'Once You Pop, You Can't Stop'.

## Should your primary line be a pun?

There's no reason why it can't be, although tread with caution—as I mentioned in the previous names chapter—puns can add charm, warmth, and humour to cold copy, but they can also come off a little cheesy on occasion. Wordplay can help people remember the line, so it can be valuable but because your brand's primary line is intended to last a very long time, you must be prepared to live with it for a while. There are puns and there are puns, some are clever and subtle, others not so much.

House of Fraser uses the pun-based line 'Temptation on every level' and this works well because this brand is widely known as a department store. I also like the strapline of the jewellery brand Kay the jeweller that runs: 'Every kiss begins with Kay' because it's clever, subtle, and paints a charming yet relevant "Picture of Benefit" to its audience.

Beware of putting the operative word of your pun in quotation marks, for example, if your brand makes bratwurst sausage, you could consider the line 'Don't fear the wurst' but please don't write 'Don't fear the "wurst"' as that's the written equivalent of winking and nudging someone to highlight an innuendo. TESCO ran a brand-partner press campaign for Durex—essentially selling cut-price condoms—and the advert featured packshots under the line 'More bang for your buck.' Wisely, the word bang was not put in quotation marks.

We all love a pun, deep down, but it usually pays to play safe and reserve puns for short-term campaigns with specific products—which they can always axe if they need to—rather than in top-level long-term "parent brand" straplines. For example, Costa Coffee provides complementary napkins that read 'Better latte than never.' Puns seem to work very well with food-based brands: 'Shrimply the best, 'Kale Caesar', 'Penne for your thoughts'...

## Mirror, with a twist

Another way to approach the creation of your brand's line is to present the central truth of the key end-user benefit, using the mirroring of words or themes. This can create interestingly ironic and seemingly paradoxical lines that make you stop and think. This is a form of wordplay that can make a line very engaging and memorable, but not quite as overt or "cheeky" as a pun.

For example:

*'I am stuck on Band-Aid 'cause Band-Aid's stuck on me!'* (*Band-Aid*).

*'Loves the jobs you hate'* (*Mr Muscle*).

*'It takes a tough man to make a tender chicken'* (*Perdue*, US chicken producer).

*'If It Matters To You, It Matters To Us'* (*Herald*, US newspaper).

*'Have a Break, Have a KitKat'* (*KitKat*).

'*The World's Local Bank*' (*HSBC*).

'I float like a butterfly, sting like a bee.' (Muhammed Ali)

'I'm not a businessman; I'm a business, man.' (Jay-Z)

'It's not the size of the dog in the fight, it's the size of the fight in the dog.' (Mark Twain)

## The power of three

Three is the magic number.

When a pair's too little and a foursome's too many, ladies and gentlemen: the trio, the triad, the triumvirate.

People just seem to like things better when they're served up as a threesome.

Goldilocks, how many bears? Shakespeare, how many witches? How many little pigs? How many Billy Goats Gruff? How many Musketeers? How many people of a certain nationality walk into a bar? Three. Three. Three.

Throughout history, messages, jokes, and soundbites of great importance seem to resonate better when they're presented in trios.

The line of Julius Caesar? 'I came, I saw, I conquered'

The line of the French Revolution? 'Liberté, égalité, fraternité!'

The founding line of Brand America? 'Life, liberty and the pursuit of happiness.'

There is even a Latin phrase 'omne trium perfectum' which translates as 'everything that comes in a three is perfect'.

We see it in public announcement slogans for road safety 'Stop, Look and Listen' and counter-terrorism 'See it, say it, sorted.'

And of course, this rule is used to great effect in the lines of famous brands:

'Snap, Crackle, Pop' (Rice Krispies).

'Grace, Space, Pace' (Jaguar).

'Movers need shakers' (Foxtons).

> Many say you need a minimum of three pieces of information to tell a joke i.e. two pieces to establish a pattern, and a third to break that pattern— however, it is just about possible to establish and break a pattern with only two words, for example, Miss Piggy's brilliant 'Pretentious, Moi?' Although this does rely on the audience knowing her character—isolated without that context, the line may confuse.

## Is a line absolutely necessary and should you stay faithful to just the one line?

No and not necessarily. Your brand's top-level line is a key foundational pillar that can add tremendous value, however, it is not a "load-bearing" pillar. By this, I mean if you were to neglect to include a line, your brand would not collapse.

This is perhaps the most optional of all the eight steps, however, if you do employ a line of some kind—and I highly recommend you do—it is good to be consistent with it where possible, as this will help overall brand recognition and the more famous it becomes, the less someone can copy it.

A good DURABLE line helps to clarify your brand. And once you have one well-defined sequence of words, it pays to consistently reproduce that line ad infinitum, which is also very helpful for SEO* reasons.

However, variety is the spice of life, and if you're an exciting FMCG brand with a well-established presence in its marketplace—you can afford to keep things interesting with multiple campaign-based advertising lines and slogans. This can also be a good idea if you want to stay topical and "disruptive" or need to create alternative straplines to position spin-off products.

A good example of such a brand is the famous rum producer Bacardi. It has run with many effective lines over the years, including 'You know when it's Bacardi', 'You in?', 'Welcome to the Latin Quarter' and 'Live like you mean it'. The stronger your brand's presence in the marketplace, the greater licence and latitude it earns and the more creative its communications can become.

## Lines are more flexible than names

The good news for all brand founders and brand managers is that when it comes to operating in overseas markets, and addressing translation issues, there is much more leeway with lines than there is with names. A brand's line can be translated and reworded if necessary to better suit its new language and culture, whereas a name is—in most cases—more fixed, and locked up and styled into the primary brand identity.

With lines—as long as you ensure the translation results in a new line that conveys a message as close to the original spirit and meaning as possible—you can afford to make adjustments.

There have been some recorded instances of unfortunate strapline translations, for example when PepsiCo translated its 'Come alive with Pepsi' campaign message in Chinese, it was read by many locals as 'Pepsi brings your ancestors back from the dead.' And when the famous line of US-chicken supplier Perdue was translated for Spanish audiences, the wording read in Spanish as 'It takes an aroused man to make a chicken affectionate'.

Amen, Brother.

* Search Engine Optimization. The process of using copy (i.e. words) to enhance the way search engines (such as *Google*) appraise, list and position your online Touchpoints so you can better serve your audiences.

## Go now and create your line

We've done a lot of work, Buddy. You've built up a rich picture so far, and you're almost ready to start the exciting work of actually creating a tangible identity for your brand. But before you start sourcing graphic designers, let's formulate that one line that's going to land perfectly with your end-user and take your brand to great heights of success.

**Start formulating your line by downloading the worksheet at: giveyourselfabrand.com/findyourline**

## STEP 6

# Give your brand an identity

How do people **identify** you?

## What is a brand identity and why do you need one?

We're here, people. We've made it—to the best bit—and now it's time to start making things real.

We've established your why. Articulated your ethos. We've thought about your end-user. Given you a name, and you have just decided on the line that will communicate your brand to the world.

Now, we need to show the world what you look like.

We need to take all the valuable information we've built so far and start to think about developing your brand's identity.

But first, let's remind ourselves what a brand's identity is.

A brand identity is the definitive distinctive identifying feature—or features—that a brand uses to identify itself. And of course, that identity can then be used by your audience to help it find you.

It's badge-making time.

And pretty soon, when you see your badge, or 'brand', you are going to feel like things are finally coming together.

So, a brand can have a variety of identifying features but its primary identity is usually a logo, also known as its 'trademark' or 'brand mark'.

Now, a brand doesn't always *have* to have a logo. You may be a valuable brand *without* a logo, for example, an internationally recognised actor can be a 'brand'*. If you are an Olympic athlete it could be the distinctive pose you strike on the completion of every race. Or maybe you're a radio star, so perhaps you have a "trademark voice".

The more impression your brand makes on its audience in a certain way, the more that impression will come to be considered an underlying aspect of your brand identity.

But for most brands, the primary identity is, and should be, a static two-dimensional visual trademark.

Of course, the primary identity could also be an animated or 3D trademark. If, for example, you are a film company you could have an audio-visual identity in the form of a short animated 'sting'—usually an animation with some sound effect or musical phrase. And if you are

* But celebrities should consider creating an actual logo, or trademark, even if it's their signature—because it's easier to protect a copyrighted trademark than it is your face or your pose. (The US actor Frank Sivero tried to sue the creators of The Simpsons because he felt the show used his likeness to create the character 'Louie'. The case was dismissed, however, I would not advise using someone else's face—without their permission—as your brand's identity or to promote your goods and services. Just a good rule of thumb.)

creating content such as adverts, podcasts, or programs for TV, web, or radio it's often wise to create an audio identity to sit next to your logo.

But in the first instance, for the vast majority, the primary identity is a non-animated logo that can be printed anywhere—and that is most certainly what we are talking about here.

A logo is powerful.

A powerful device to captivate, engage, differentiate, build trust, signal professionalism and credibility, and maintain consistency across Touchpoints.

A logo, or trademark, uses shapes and colour to create a meaningful, and recognisable, arrangement that can be read by speakers of all languages.

In most cases, it is usually a typographic treatment—that is to say, the logo features words.

And these words are usually your brand name, and maybe your brand line—working as a team, with a distinctive emblem or icon. However, some primary identities are purely iconic, without any need for their name, and can be identified on the strength of an icon alone. For example the distinctive golden arches of McDonald's*, the bitten fruit† of the Apple brand, the swoosh of Nike, or the green mermaid of Starbucks. But these are, of course, examples of well-established identities that have evolved over many years. In fact all four did start initially with the brand names clearly included in their identities.

So this is where you take your name and your line, and you make your mark.

'But why do I need an identity?' asks Uncle Brian. 'Why can't I just stick up a name and a website and maybe a mobile phone number?'

Because, Brian, a brand needs an identity to bring everything together. Into one family, under one roof, to claim ownership of the assets and Touchpoints, goods, and services it produces and renders. To say, 'This asset belongs to us'.

It's helpful to see your primary identity as the badge, seal, or stamp you apply to everything you do, to say 'We did this. This is our work.'

If you invent a new custard: you put your logo on the packaging, the adverts, the shelf-labels, and delivery lorries. Why do you do this? So your customers can find your custard again and again, develop a

* 'Golden arches' is the popular phrase that denotes McDonald's distinctive signage but it was the actual term used by its architect Stanley Clark Meston when they presented their initial prototypes in 1952.

† Apparently the bitemark distinguishes an apple from a cherry.

relationship, and begin the precious process of developing trust in your goods and services.

If you have a crane rental company, you put your logo on all your cranes for the same reason, 'this is one of our cranes.' Plus it gives you free advertising. You just don't get that reach with a mobile phone number alone.

Logos themselves are central to the philosophy, practice, and history of branding. The word 'brand' means to 'burn' and the first recorded acts of branding were when cattle farmers would use a hot iron (or 'brand') to physically burn (or 'brand') a logo (or 'brand') onto their cows. To identify them and to say, in no uncertain terms, 'This is my cow, people!'.

Branding is, after all, really just a contrived association between things. It's representational: this means that. This logo means 'good cows', and that one means 'tasty custard'.

The famous designer Paul Rand said that 'a logo gets its meaning from the quality of the thing it represents, not the other way around.'

I would agree with this to a certain extent—if the greengrocer is good, you will come to associate his logo with the good things in life, no matter how shoddy his logo is, and if the greengrocer is bad, and always selling you rotten vegetables, you'll come to associate his logo with the bad things, no matter how good his logo looks.

But even so, any association between two things is a two-way street, and a primary identity is still probably the most prized and valuable piece of any brand's equity. If a logo is professionally produced and well-considered it says to people 'These guys are professional and consider things well'.

Because we humans are intelligent sophisticated 'thin-slicers'* able to gauge a great deal from a little information, a logo can say a lot about a brand in a short space of time.

And so, it certainly pays to employ a professional graphic designer to create or at least help create, your primary identity. An identity that once created will require zero maintenance cost and will continue to deliver value and return on investment for the lifetime of your brand, travelling the world for you like a silent tireless ambassador, while you sleep like a baby.

* For more on 'thin-slicing' in general I recommend the book *Blink: The Power of Thinking Without Thinking* (2005) by Malcolm Gladwell.

Having an identity to look at and hold up to the world is a significant turning point and a big psychological boost. So it's now time to turn a big corner in the branding process and create something you'll love for a long time. This chapter covers all the things you'll need to think about when developing your identity.

## What makes a good brand identity?

There are identities and there are identities. There are a lot of identities. And in this context, I mean logos. Some logos are recognisable the world over, and others have been designed in the last hour. Some are brilliant, some not so much. Some are loved by one person and hated by another. Like any piece of graphic design—or indeed any feature of the universe—they will be perceived differently by different people. And so, there is no such thing as a perfect logo. However, some logos work better than others and there are key things to consider to ensure your logo does the job it needs to do.

A logo is a symbol—a piece of visual data—a meaningful mark, designed to convey meaning to a certain audience. The primary role of your logo is to identify your brand and its offerings to its audience. Logos are audience-specific, so before you design your logo, you need to have a good idea of who your audience is and you must know that it will understand the meaning of the logo. That's why we looked at your end-user before this step.

A logo is a connection between a brand and its audience. The meaning behind the logo—or symbol—is assumed to be understood by both parties; and if the audience is confused, it's either an incorrect or as yet uneducated audience looking at it, or the brand has failed. Your designer must design accordingly. The better you know your audience—and what your audience understands, and wants from life—the better you can craft the right identity.

It's also important to run some due diligence on the other logos already existing, to check yours is unique. It is very common for a designer to develop an identity only to find a very similar one already exists. Avoiding such unintentional duplication previously required encyclopedic knowledge with painstaking attention to logo directories and a good degree of luck. But now that Google has launched its 'Search by image' feature, one can simply check one's logo idea against similar finds. This is by no means a fail-safe check but it's a very powerful and effective tool, and worth 20 minutes of your time if it can help you avoid embarrassment, expense, or legal action later.

---

'The only mandate in logo design is that they be distinctive, memorable and clear.'
*Paul Rand*

---

As you can see, I like to quote Paul Rand—he was a brilliant and highly influential American graphic designer who designed the famous identities of IBM, ABC, and UPS. These logos all became registered trademarks.

His remark above is almost perfect, but I would argue a logo should also be evocative and be designed with consideration to what thoughts and feelings it could evoke in the hearts and minds of its audience. Also, what does 'clear' mean? Based on these ideas, I have developed the **R.U.D.E.** system, which states that a good logo should be:

**Robust**
**Unique**
**Distinctive**
**Evocative**

The RUDE system is not a step-by-step process for creating a primary identity, it is simply a way to test your primary identity and any options created on the way to perfecting your primary identity. The process of creating a brand's primary identity is specialist work that requires a trained and creative graphic designer but having the RUDE acronym in mind when reviewing options can be very handy.

When reviewing design options your first filter should be your own feelings—i.e. how much you like the logo—and also how well you feel the proposed option is suited to your brand. You only need to run the "RUDE test" on identity options you're happy to proceed with.

## Your logo should be Robust

'What on earth does Robust mean?'

It means your logo should be a strong and recognisable mark that could be reproduced anywhere, from a tiny postage stamp to a massive corn circle. It should make sense within its own little world and feature balanced elements that work well together. Robust means solid, clean, and simple.

Your identity can—and most certainly should—feature colour, and any colour you like, because colour is valuable in life and especially so in brand identity, however, it should be able to work first in black only.

When I am designing an identity, I first design it as a monochrome flat-colour treatment that could be cut out of a potato, and printed onto a tree. I only look at colours later, after the initial work of shape creation and element arrangement has taken place.

If the logo works first in one colour you can be confident it will work using multiple colours and tints down the line. It may even take a gradient between two colours, which could be useful from a brand differentiation viewpoint.

A brand identity often has to work across a wide spectrum of applications, so robustness is vital. Your logo should feature balanced relationships between all its constituent parts with as much thought given to the space that shapes don't take up as the space that they do.

Your logo is a visual poem told in one succinct graphical hit. Whether it's a purely typographic affair, centred around your brand name—or a combination of both type and symbol—every element must preside in consideration of every other element. Your logo should be a shining presentation of balanced relationships, not a "dog's breakfast" of rushed typography and embarrassed shapes.

Consider how it works as a whole. Don't get distracted by one element over another. If your logo features your brand name in an Ultra Light typeface below an unwieldy icon—like an image of a hippopotamus—your name may get completely overshadowed and ignored or seen as mud—as well as running the risk of being potentially swallowed up by ink if it were ever to be reversed out of a dark coloured background.

Good designers always work within a feedback loop that ensures a logo is "sense-checked" at various stages of its development. Often this is done many times before the client—in this case, you—sees it, and of course, various waves of amends follow after the client has become involved in the process.

Testing a logo during development is a prudent and effective measure to ensure robustness. Limit your "review board" to a sensible number, everyone will have an opinion if asked for one.

## Your logo should be Unique

Your brand's primary identity should be unlike any other.

It can have the feel of other brands if it wishes to be perceived like other trusted brands in its space, however, for legal reasons, your brand identity should be unique and not look too much like another. The exact legalities on this differ from country to country but ultimately these laws are similar and in place to prevent trademark confusion, copyright infringement, and counterfeiting.

In the UK, if your brand's logo looks like that of another brand to the point of being deemed an attempted replica, and/or the replica logo is used to sell items by misrepresentation—such as a counterfeit garment or product bearing the replica logo of another established brand—a seller can be prosecuted under the Trademark Counterfeiting Act of 1984.

If your brand's logo is not knowingly copying—or 'passing off' as—another brand, but still coincidentally appears to be very similar to another established brand identity, it is still likely you are infringing on the other brand's copyright. Even if this is accidental, you can expect to receive communications from their lawyers, usually in the initial form of a 'cease and desist' notice—asking you to take down the logo from public view—which if you ignore could result in further legal action, as they may have a good case to sue you. This could be a very costly blow to your brand.

The likelihood of two independent brands coming up with the same name and a very similar mark is small but very possible—after all, names tend to influence the logos they become part of—so the more research you or your graphic designer does to ensure your logo is Unique, the better.

### Your logo should be Distinctive

As mentioned above, your logo should be Unique but it should also be Distinctive—it should catch the eye and stand out. Distinctive identities sear themselves in the eyes of those who see them and stick better in the mind and memory. When your end-user is going about their day, they should be able to hold your identity in their memory, so they know what to look for, and so if they see it, should instantly recognise it as representing your brand.

The primary identity of the coffee shop brand Starbucks—which features a figurehead of a mermaid with flowing hair—is a great example of a distinctive mark. Whenever you see it, you know it is representing a bone fide Starbucks outlet—had the brand gone for something like a coffee bean icon, the mark would have been less distinctive. Other examples of distinctive identities include: the Tesla brand mark, with its distinctive 'T' emblem, the Adidas logo with its distinctive three-pronged symbol, and the mark of Lacoste with its distinctive crocodile icon.

### Your logo should be Evocative

Your logo should evoke thoughts, feelings, and associations in its audiences. The thoughts, feelings, and associations triggered by a brand identity in the minds—and hearts—of its audience will ultimately come to be attached to that identity, however, most brand identities feature icons or symbols with pre-existing associations—such as the Lacoste crocodile i.e. the Lacoste emblem was not the first time humanity saw a depiction of a crocodile. In contrast, a minority of brand identities create an arbitrary symbol that has never been seen before—such as the badge of Mercedes-Benz or the post-1998 three-striped mark of Adidas—and also the pre-1998 trefoil icon of Adidas.

> Many distinctive brand logos are built on pre-existing symbols already freighted with meaning e.g. the McDonald's 'M' was an original design but based on the pre-existing letterform of 'M'; and the apple of Apple was an original design but based on an 'apple' icon. Humanity has a long history of sharing symbols and while there are wide overlaps of common agreement as to the meaning conveyed by a certain symbol there is by no means a definitive library of set meanings. So when developing your logo it is important to consider your audience and the wider implications of whatever your proposed symbol means. One group may associate wings with freedom, but another might associate wings with tyranny.

Whether your brand identity/logo is built using depictions of symbols with pre-existing meanings or brand-new symbols without any prior meaning, you should be aware of the thoughts, feelings, and associations it is triggering in your intended audiences. A symbol or mark can be a powerful means of stirring emotions, so you must be confident it's stirring the right ones.

Always ask: 'What is this evoking?'

It can be very useful and interesting to test your proposed logo on focus groups and see exactly what people think. The idea is not to see if people like it, but rather an opportunity to check for any unseen problems.

## It's also nice for a logo to feature an 'Easter egg'

'Easter eggs' are pleasant little surprises that a viewer is free to stumble across at their leisure. In the context of logos, this could take the form of an embedded feature not immediately obvious at first glance, but when seen, appears very smart and endearing. For example, the distinctive mark of the FedEx brand just looks like two words—typeset in something like Futura Bold—fused together, but if you look again you see that the designer used masterful kerning and typography to create an arrow in the negative space between the E and the x, and once you see it, you can never not see it.

Good graphic designers can play with shapes and words and, well, graphics, and design smart visual solutions that add value and charm.

The mark of BP Ultimate features an interesting little surprise, next time you look at it you may notice the logo doesn't feature an 'i'. Also, if you look at the smiling arrow in the Amazon logo you'll notice it is pointing from 'A' to 'Z' suggesting the wide range of its offering. Look at how the dot in the 'i' in the Gillette logo is 'shaven' like a hair. Look at the Baskin Robbins logo and you'll see the 'BR' actually shows a '31' which refers to its 31 flavours.

## It's also nice when your identity is economical

The simpler your identity is, the more Robust it is. However creating a simple identity that is also Unique, Distinctive and that Evokes what you want it to evoke, is not easy.

It may look easy and the finished design may appear simple, but if you like it and it does the job and it is RUDE, then do not mistake simplicity for ineffectiveness.

Things that appear simple can often fool us into thinking they didn't require much thought or take much creative time but any fool can make something complicated. To make something simple takes skill.

Most good design is the result of an intelligent thought process that works out what needs to go where and why. Good logo design is a conversation with shape and usually a process of creation, experiment, and distillation—boiling down a logo to the point where it says all it needs to say in the most elegant way possible, without any loss in function.

---

'A designer knows he has achieved perfection
not when there is nothing left to add,
but when there is nothing left to take away.'
*Antoine de Saint-Exupéry*

---

## Don't forget the submark

A submark is a "boiled down" version of your primary identity designed to be used in places where the use of the full primary logo would be impractical. Submarks are often used as favicons—those little branded squares that sit on the top tab of your website—and as icons representing your brand, which can be useful for apps, emojis, and other small widgets. Submarks can also serve as subtle 'secondary identities' to use when you want to 'brand' something but feel your full logo would be a touch too much. For example as a feature on your menus, uniforms, stationery, or monogrammed towels.

'Oh, George, look, they've got monogrammed towels! We're coming back here.'

Submarks are usually created as an afterthought when the main logo has already been designed. However, consideration of your submark from the outset can enhance the overall design process of your primary identity as it impels you to think about what the most distinctive aspects of your logo are, how everything fits together to make it pop, and whether anything can be added or taken away.

The process of designing a logo is largely a process of research, sketching, experimentation, and refinement through the distillation of elements.

Seeing your identity as a group of elements that can be rearranged or simplified if necessary, rather than one fixed element, can help the creation process. Ultimately, a submark gives your brand greater bandwidth across the many Touchpoint options available.

## Give your brand identity colour

A strong brand identity should be RUDE, and in the first instance should work as a black-only version to ensure it can be reproduced in the most hostile of environments. However, colour is such an important and valuable feature of our physical world—it would be plain stupid not to harness its power to full effect in your brand's identity and your brand's style.

Colour, like many aspects of shared human experience, is just another idea, but one we tend to solidly agree upon as a very meaningful part of physical existence. It is created in our minds by appreciating different wavelengths of light in the visible spectrum. The conditions for appreciating these wavelengths are variable but experts believe there are approximately around 10 million possible variations, and so 10 million unique colours available to the average human eye. But because we humans like to reduce and group information where possible—to make things shareable —we've "bucketed" the 10 million or so down to a more manageable number.

A nice round ten.

The ten colours most people will collectively agree upon are black, white, grey, red, orange, yellow, green, blue, indigo and violet.

There is some evidence to suggest some colours were agreed upon and accepted before others. For example, it is believed the concept of red is older than the concept of blue. I'm not completely sure about this, seeing as the sky is blue, sometimes—however, there is a lot of evidence to show that blues and violets were the latest of the ten to be effectively reproduced as a colour. Nowadays we take it for granted when we see purple soft furnishings but for centuries this colour eluded us, its pigments not so accessible. Unlike the reds, browns, blacks, yellows, and greens that occur in nature, in rocks, on the ground, and in the flora, and fauna of yesteryear's everyday life. This is why purple was for a long time associated with wealth and status, and perhaps why light blue is thought of as a spiritual peace-loving colour.

But it's easy to see why red is thought of as the oldest and boldest on the spectrum. On the most primordial level, red remains powerful, dangerous, bold. An exciting colour. Blood. Passion. Ladybirds. The earliest human art: cave paintings, were created in reds and earthly browns—mainly because these were the most available of colours, but also maybe because the cavemen found them "homely", the kind of palette that goes well with scatter cushions. Great taste never goes out of fashion.

There are, of course, many more. Humanity has built up a secondary palette of thousands—including such wonderful hues as tangerine, khaki, charcoal, maroon, turquoise, obsidian, silver, azure, turmeric, salmon, mulberry, mauve, burgundy, saffron, and greige. Not to mention Victorian Skies. But these are more likely to cause argument among people unless they have a PANTONE swatch book handy.

'The best colour in the whole world
is the one that looks good on you.'
*Coco Chanel*

## What colour will you have?

Many famous brands are associated with just one colour, for example, Coca-Cola (red) and easyJet (orange). Some are associated with two colours. Pepsi (red and blue). FedEx (purple and orange). Some are associated with three: Burger King (blue, yellow, and red) and LIDL with its blue, yellow, and red). And some brands even attempt four colours. Microsoft (red, green, blue, and yellow) and Google (blue, red, yellow and green).

With the possible exception of Google—which famously uses white space to great effect—I would say there's a "reverse correlation" between a brand's visual potency and the number of colours it uses in its primary palette. That is to say, the more colours you add the less distinctive and impressive your brand becomes.

(In the Style section we will look a bit further at how to manage colours across your brand's touchpoints, but the decisions you make when creating your brand's identity will influence your brand's style, so read the Style section too, before making any final decisions on colour at the logo stage.)

## What about typography?

Most likely, your brand's primary identity is going to feature your name—certainly for the first few years while you establish yourself (before you become as famous as Nike or Starbucks)—and so: your identity is going to feature a word, or words, and so it will feature alphabetic characters.

We humans use character-based languages to communicate. And most brand identities require characters, such as letters, commas, and numerals. English, for example, has a limited pool of just 26 letters, plus a few other characters like this unnecessary & (ampersand).

These characters can be reproduced any way you like to create words and convey meaning but thanks to Johannes Gutenberg's invention of moveable type in the fifteenth century—allowing us humans the ability to duplicate the printed word in large volumes, and thanks to the technological "domino chain" that followed, including the invention of the computer and Desktop Publishing (DTP)—you are now able to read this paragraph as typed characters which belong to the typeface 'Sabon'.

How you choose to design, arrange, and use these typefaces is a process—and an art—called typography. And typography is essentially, the selection—or creation—of fonts and how you choose to arrange them.

---

'Typography is what language looks like.'
*Ellen Lupton*

---

> Typography is a key consideration in identity design and can be used effectively to position your brand. Typography is also a key factor in your brand's style too—so definitely read the Style section before you commit to your logo design.

## Which font?

When it comes to choosing which fonts and typefaces* will best suit your brand, there are many to choose from, and your Graphic Designer (who I will now for evermore refer to as 'GD') will be able to advise or shortlist options. Your GD may even propose custom-designing a completely new typeface, or even a new font set, to better suit your brand, although this could incur more design time/cost.

To give you a very quick overview of a few typeface styles and fonts out there to consider here is a cursory breakdown of font categories—I'll be fast and loose as this isn't a technical Typographer's Manual, just an overview:

*Serif fonts:*

Serif fonts are typefaces that feature little bits on the ends of the letters.† These are generally considered 'classic' fonts and are widely used for body copy as they are believed to be easier to read in smaller sizes. This is a serif font.

*Sans Serif fonts:*

'Sans' is French for 'without', so these are fonts 'without serifs', i.e. no little bits on the ends of the letters. These are generally considered 'modern' fonts and are widely used for headlines and posters.

This is a sans-serif font.

* The word 'font' was originally used to specifically refer to an individual set of characters—the set of metal type required to make up a certain typeface, as in 'I need the metal font for that typeface called Baskerville, so I can set the letters in my type-press.'

However, thanks mostly to the advent and uptake of computers and DTP—and the actual means of getting a typeface to appear on your computer application—the word 'font' now means the computer file required to reproduce the particular typeface in the application. So fonts are now actually software—i.e. code-based programs—and yet in our modern workplaces the word 'font' has now come to mean 'typeface', as in 'I need the font Avenir, and so I will just use this drop-down menu to select it.'

Typographers are the originators we should thank for creating the actual typefaces, to begin with, however, coders or coding programs are required to digitalise and code the typefaces into fonts.

So really the meaning of the words hasn't changed. The typeface is, and always was, the actual 'design' of the typeface—i.e. the design of the set of letterforms and the distinctive shape of its characters and glyphs (The word 'glyph' is mostly used nowadays to refer to the additional characters outside the 26 English characters, such as !, @, #, and $, however, the characters A-Z were, and still are in many places, also called 'glyphs').

And the 'font' is, and always was, the means of getting that typeface onto a touchpoint in the real world. However, you don't necessarily need to know all this if you have a good graphic designer in your corner, as they should be able to handle all your typography-related needs and questions.

† The little bits on the ends are the 'serifs'.

*Script fonts:*

*Script fonts tend to be used for highly-stylised work because their decorative flowing strokes are based on old fashioned writing and calligraphy styles. Creating effective pieces of typography—or typographical 'lock-ups' as they're sometimes known—using script fonts requires careful handling. People often use these fonts and make the mistake of writing out a poster or newsletter headline in CAPITAL LETTERS.* **I LOVE USING CAPITAL LETTERS —ALSO KNOWN AS UPPER-CASE LETTERS—ESPECIALLY IN SANS SERIF 'SWISS' FONTS** because they look great on posters, *HOWEVER IN A SCRIPTY FONT THE EFFECT IS NOT QUITE BEAUTIFUL.*

*'Handwritten' fonts:*

*'Handwritten' fonts are fonts that have been designed to look as if they've been written in pen i.e. by hand. They can be very effective for creating a relaxed and casual style. This is one example. This is another. And this is another.*

As well as these general distinctions, you also have additional stylings that can be applied to any kind of font, as most DTP and design apps allow you to override the font's default appearance and also make the font:

*Italic:* i.e. making the font appear slanted or drunk. This is useful for a variety of reasons and is often used to pull out keywords in a block of text, such as brand names like for example *Colgate, NASA* and *MTV.*

**Bold:** i.e. making the font appear thicker and heavier, well, bolder—this is the typographic equivalent of 'you wanna go large with that typeface?'

***Weight and size:*** Colour and italics aside, working fonts usually go by the two guiding parameters of weight and size. 'Weight' relates to the thickness of the letters i.e. how heavy or light the letters appear, and 'size' of course relates to the size of the letters i.e. how big they appear, and how much space the letters take up and how many words you can fit on a line. Increasing the weight of a font does also have an incremental effect on how much space a letter takes up but not as much as changing the size.

In terms of weight, a font will usually be available in a range of weights, and this will usually be disclosed in the font's name e.g.

**Baskerville SemiBold** or ***Baskerville BoldItalic***.

A font's size is typically measured by a unit called a 'point' (and abbreviated to 'pt') and this body copy you are reading now is actually 11pt (in 'Sabon Regular').

When a type foundry releases a new font, they will usually release it in a range of weights and this set of weights is known as a 'family'.

You can usually get a discount for buying a whole family, as opposed to just one weight—like when you get a discount for buying wine by the bottle rather than by the glass.

Due to the way that most computers handle the fonts these days, fonts used for DTP and print purposes require a different file type to fonts intended for use in websites, however this is probably a level of technical detail you can leave to your GD.

In fact, when it comes to typography, it does pay to leave as much to your GD as possible. A good GD can do wonderful things with obscure overlooked fonts, and a bad GD can make popular fonts look awful. 'Great typography is the beautiful arrangement of type, not the arrangement of beautiful type'.

That said, certain typefaces—or fonts—do bring certain inherent characteristics to the table. The font Comic Sans is always going to look like it's been taken from a comic book or graphic novel and Baskerville is always going to have little flourishes called serifs.

When you are choosing your fonts—or creating or reviewing the typographic pieces created from your chosen fonts—the key questions to ask yourself are:

- Do I like it?
- Is it legible?
- Is this helping to make my brand identity RUDE?

---

'Words have meaning. Type has spirit.
The combination is spectacular.'
*Paula Scher*

---

## Time to find a good GD (Graphic Designer)

So far, the advice and exercises have been geared around doing all the grunt work yourself, after all, if you cut your own wood, you warm yourself twice. However, for this next stage, I would recommend you lay down the metaphorical axe, and use a good professional GD to create your primary identity i.e. logo.

Creating the logo is usually the first step in creating a brand's entire visual repertoire. A good logo will serve as a "keystone" for any subsequent style consideration and can influence, if not dictate, the brand's character, colour palette, typography, general visual character, and overall style.

So this is where a GD comes in very handy.

It's worth investing in a good one.

Because graphic design is important in setting up and maintaining a brand.

Graphic design is 'thinking made visual' and in the arena of branding, communication, and human affairs, 'thinking made visual' is valuable. Graphic design can 'sell' ideas, help get them past peoples' limbic systems and into the minds and hearts of your audience. Graphic design can simplify complicated information and make complex data attractive and digestible. It can reduce "informational entropy" (which I know you like doing), it can simplify the complicated and it can extract order from chaos.

Finding the essence of an idea, then compressing and expressing that in its simplest form is not easy, but if done right, can be enduringly powerful. Your logo, and the wider palette of your brand's style, communicate who your brand is and what it stands for, whether you are there or not. A good GD is the 'chef' that takes the informational ingredients of your brand's Content and transforms them into beautiful touchpoints.

---

'Design is the intermediary between information
and understanding.'
*Hans Hoffmann, painter*

---

## How to find a GD

Choose your GD with care. It's worth getting right. A GD who can translate your content and ideas into exactly what you want can be super valuable.

You may be tempted to do the design yourself—especially if your budgets are tight and you fancy yourself an artist. But consider this carefully. Even if you are a talented GD yourself, the time it takes to craft a good logo could be put to better use elsewhere, and having the fresh perspective of another brain always produces valuable insights that can unlock wonderful things.

Fostering good relationships with one or more GDs is a very worthwhile pursuit, no matter who you are.

But tread lightly. Having a good working relationship is a delicate balance. On the one hand, you want a proven professional who you can trust but you want someone you can change if necessary. So start any new working relationship with a good vetting process, some due diligence, and an exit strategy. If they consistently fail to meet your requirements you may need to look for an alternative option, so if you are thinking of using a friend or acquaintance then really make sure you know they can do a good job—for the budget you have—before you brief them.

We live in the wonderful "Age of the Internet", so good people are never too far away, there are plenty of .com websites such as Fiverr, Upwork, and 99designs that offer logo designs from GDs around the world. These days, your GD needn't be geographically proximate. We have Skype, Office365, GoogleApps, and a whole raft of online resources that enable you to communicate, brief people, brainstorm, review, amend, annotate, and proof designs, so location is becoming less and less relevant.

Your GD could be down the road or on the other side of the world. As long as you've both got a means of communication, a good internet connection and they are delivering the work—inside a legal payment system that satisfies your respective governments and tax laws—then you are off to the races.

We have social media. We have LinkedIn. We have Facebook. We have WhatsApp.

Connection and communication have never been easier however it's probably best to avoid social media to brief people. Referable email threads—that you can both keep a record of—are perhaps the best means of communication and project management.

But even if you're not directly connected to a GD, you probably know someone that is. You may have been using someone already for years, someone at your local High Road printers who designs flyers and business cards but that doesn't mean they have the skills to find and create your perfect identity.

Logo design is a fine art, so shop around.

You may work in marketing and you may already use a GD or a Graphic Design agency, but again keep in mind a good exit strategy. It's ok if you don't like what they produce, but you must tell them. Never use a logo you don't like, just to be polite. 'I don't have the heart to tell her I don't like it, and she lives next door. I'll have to face her every day, what should I do?'

Often the best way to test out a new working relationship with a GD is through a logo project, so this is an ideal opportunity to find someone who flicks your switches. The logo is a great place to start building your "Brand Support Dream Team". There may be some "teething problems"—few jobs run smoothly—but this is your opportunity to discern any issues with communication, interpretation, or working arrangements.

---

'Don't use your next-door neighbour to design your logo,
even if the very fate of the universe depends on it.'
*Anon*

---

## Writing the brief

One of the key benefits of the Give yourself a brand system is that whether you knew it or not, you have been writing the brief for your brand's new identity by following the steps so far. And now, all you need to do is download the GYAB identity brief template—available at giveyourselfabrand.com/id-brief (QR code on page 168).

All you need to do is fill out the questions and hand the brief to your GD and have them do the rest. Having such a clear and well-defined articulation of your brand's reason-for-being (your why), your way-of-being (your ethos), your end-user profile, and of course your name and line, is pure gold for the logo creation process. It will save hours of consultation time and will eliminate the typical confusion and misunderstandings that haunt so many logo-based projects.

Naturally, you may have additional requirements, thoughts, and recommendations to give to your GD—in relation to colour preferences or typefaces, etc.; the small details that can make all the difference—but these can, of course, be added where necessary. A good GD will be able to discern the important details from the background information.

## Learning to speak design

In logo design, we create something from nothing—'aliquid ex nihilo', as the Romans said—so it can be difficult to talk about, or refer to, something that doesn't exist. In this environment of uncertainty and opportunity, it is therefore important that everyone involved practices good thinking, patience, empathy, and clear communication.

I worked as a GD for fifteen years, and I've heard some things said by clients during the logo design/development process. Obviously, a good GD should take on board anything a client says to them, and be able to wisely interpret or diplomatically question anything that isn't obvious or logical but a good brief is more like a conversation than an edict. And you, as a client, can help the process—and save time and money—by first considering how you frame feedback to your GD.

For example, don't say things like 'Can you make it more visual?'

Such an instruction is not that helpful. I was once given that instruction from a client, and after some digging, I discovered they just wanted some icons placed by the text. Had they said: 'Could we try some more icons by the text?' it would have saved five hours of work. I've had clients say 'We don't want to use red, or blue, or purple but we want a similar colour like that. What is there?'

Everyday, GDs around the world are expected to decipher—and work with—ambiguous and poorly considered instructions. Don't add to their burden. GDs are usually creative, polite, empathetic, and seasoned to bad briefing, but that doesn't mean they've gotten any better at deciphering it. And because many GDs are creative and polite, they'll often try and solve a problem on their own, over many hours, when you could have solved it for them in about five minutes.

When you use a GD, you should put yourself in their position and ask 'Would I understand this?' because ultimately, this helps you. Saving time and pain on the logo saves money and maintains the relationship with your GD. Naturally, the GD is the professional in the situation and the obligation and burden of understanding often falls to them to guide and manage the process, but as a client, you do have a vested interest in thinking about how you are briefing the job, how you are reviewing any submitted work and how you are articulating your responses in ways that get your concerns and preferences understood. A GD is usually happy to charge for any wasted time—so you owe it to yourself to think about how you are briefing and giving feedback because it streamlines and speeds up the process and you'll get to your ideal identity sooner.

> If you like something, say so, if you don't like something, say why you don't like it. But even if something is incorrect, be patient, and reflective and use it as a reference point. Even bad designs provide value, in that they at least show—in a concrete and referable way—an example of what not to do.

In the visual arts, anything that already exists is referable and therefore: valuable. Do not be overly polite to your GD, but do not be overtly rude either, they are probably—hopefully—trying their best. The only RUDE thing about the process should be the logo that comes out of it.

Good logo design requires a good understanding of the brief and a thorough exploration of the options that arise from the creative process.

Great logo design often requires a degree of nerve, waiting for a brilliant visual idea that often likes to evade all but the most persistent.

A visual idea that in some profound way reflects a vital aspect of your brand's "DNA". If the entire process can be marshalled by a visionary GD who can steer the project away from a paltry compromise towards a classic logo that outlives us all, then so much the better.

You can say anything you want to your GD, but to get the best out of them, consider the communicational payload of your responses: be clear, be direct, and use adjectives and nouns that actually help. Give them space and time but also clear parameters, feedback, and deadlines.

## How long should a logo take to design?

Much like any bespoke project, the time it takes will depend on the overall requirement and the agreed-upon terms your GD has advised. Ultimately, your GD should recommend and advise timings, review stages, and submissions to suit you both. The important thing to remember is that this is a very important part of your brand building, so you must get it right. Because when you do get it right—and you'll know it when you see it—your brand's logo will serve you ceaselessly day and night wherever it is seen.

It is a key investment.

The logo is a big opportunity and if you create a brilliant one, you attain the power to thrust your brand's profile into the stratosphere.

The thing about good graphic design is that it can be time-consuming. What the GD is essentially doing is creating something brand new that didn't exist before, and that usually requires some thought, some ideas, some sketching, and quite a bit of scrunching up paper. The GD's friend is the waste basket. Even with a great brief, and a highly prescriptive steer, it can take a while to find that elusive emblem, so it can pay to factor in a healthy "Phase One"—of two to four days (spread over a week or two). Often the best policy is to begin by creating or requesting a series of pencil-sketched options that explore a variety of iconic treatments along with a 'mood board' showcasing effects and typefaces.

"Visibility of Options" is a mantra I use with early-stage identity work, and no idea is dismissed because you never know where your logo idea is...

...hiding.

Another valuable mantra is "Embrace the Tiny Change".

Sometimes, within an idea that doesn't immediately pop with you, there hides an amazing logo, just waiting for a small tweak or a tiny change. Teasing out the small details and wrestling with visual elements and their various relationships is the long work of the GD. This is the unseen time and diligence great design requires. If graphic design is the "Poetry of Shapes", then logo design is like creating a stanza: crafting the type, tones, elements, and colours into a balanced whole. A logo is a microcosm of your brand, an ambassador for all seasons, and if done well, can outlast a lifetime—one cannot be whipped up in a lunch hour.

That said, the idea for a winning logo can come over lunch when the brain relaxes to spark inspiration. The good GD should be able to take that precious ember into the tinderbox of their care and breathe it into an eternal fire. Such imagery! I need to sit down.

## How much should a logo cost?

As with pretty much any service, there is no universal "set cost" for logo design. The value of anything usually comes down to what people are willing to pay, negotiate, and accept; value is subjective.

'My friend got a great logo designed for $100 online.'

Yes, some people do get lucky but it always pays to shop around, check out various portfolios, and get recommendations and a feel for the way a particular GD works. But essentially all graphic design is service-based, so you are paying for someone's time. More experienced GDs tend to have higher rates than less experienced GDs, however cheaper doesn't always mean worse, and cheaper doesn't always mean better. It's common, likely, and reasonable to see a GD's abilities increase with their cost but assume nothing until you've checked out portfolios and working styles. It's really about finding a GD that "gels" with your way of working, and communicating, and finding someone who can produce stuff you like.

It's about getting a good fit.

Graphic and logo design is specialised work done by a trained craftsperson and the standard cost tends to be based on a quote, which is based on an estimation of the studio time required, based on the brief.

Cost will depend on how much time is required and how much time is required will depend on the nature of your requirement, but in my experience, the work of identity design requires approximately three key stages:

1). Background work of deciding and defining what the mark should 'say' and you can do much of this yourself, in fact, you probably already have in the work we have done so far.
2). Idea phase, generation of logo options, and review
3). Refinement of idea into the finalised mark that you fall in love with

Logo design projects have to factor in briefing time, creative thinking time, plus time for designing the logo options, refining the options, and all the necessary review stages, or 'amend' stages. Plus the creation of a definitive logo set that contains all the necessary artwork-ready variants such as vector files, transparent PNGs and JPGs, etc.

Some GDs and GD agencies offer upfront package deals that may include other items beyond the identity. Some people publish—or share on request—detailed rate cards that give hourly rates or day rates.

Ultimately, there are three key things to consider:

1). Good logo design takes time.
2). A good logo is a good investment and is worth getting right.
3). If you go for the cheap option or lowest bidder you may end up spending more money on revisions and still not get what you want.

Whoever your GD is and wherever you find them and whatever they charge, you must get the cost questions discussed, defined, and agreed upon early. Never assume anything with regard to working arrangements. It's important to have all payment terms out in the open and agreed upon. Beware the GD who asks for prepayment. Prepayment should not be necessary. Prepayment suggests a defensive GD who has previously delivered work that didn't meet the brief and subsequently faced payment disputes.

You want to find a GD with a proven track record of delivering strong work within a framework of good client service and professionalism.

Costs should be clear and capped by stage and show where all review stages are included and how any additional amends or work beyond the capped stages are charged for. If you increase the scope of the brief, it's fair to expect the GD to submit a revised quote or cost guide to cover this. Your GD may negotiate a staged invoice process or a more standard arrangement where you receive the invoice following project completion, but it is not common practice to pay anything upfront.

---

'If you think good design is expensive,
you should look at the cost of bad design.'
*Ralf Speth*

---

## Do I need to give or sign any contracts?

This will depend on your preferences—and those of your GD—but as a general rule, consider contracts carefully. Always read any contract thoroughly before you sign anything, always ask for advice, and always question anything you do not fully understand. If you are ever pressured to sign anything without reading, do not sign. Better to feel a moment of embarrassment than a lifetime of regret.

If you get to a point where you're happy with a GD's portfolio, quote, and general working approach, in some cases they may send a contract your way as part of their working style, so ensure you read it carefully and know what you are signing for.

In design-related projects, an SoW (Statement of Work) is often used to define the activities, timelines, and 'deliverables' of a project. This can help to articulate the brief, crystallise expectations, and prevent any disputes down the line on both sides. But if this is something you're not comfortable with, and if for example, you do not see what benefit it brings to you, then do question it and don't be afraid to rewrite or refuse it.

## Who owns the copyright of my brand's logo?

If your GD is a paid employee of your company, the contract they are working to, most likely states that they transfer all personal copyright to your company by default. However, if they are a private contractor, this is not the case, and without any paperwork or agreements saying otherwise, copyright law almost always assigns the actual creation of an original work to the creator, not the client.

While it's unlikely a GD would ever hold you to ransom, you don't want to even be in a position where that would be possible; someone else should not have control over your identity. So, it's usually a prudent step to request the GD transfer all copyrights—or extend you unlimited usage rights—in written form. The agreement is that your GD creates your identity for payment, and as part of that arrangement, they transfer or extend full unlimited usage rights. This needs to be in writing somewhere, preferably on headed letter paper from your GD, as part of the quote process.

(If you proceeded to register your identity as a registered trademark, if successful, this trademark would belong to your brand by default, regardless of the original copyright status.)

## Should my GD sign an NDA?

This depends on your preferences. There is no general legal requirement to ask your GD to sign an NDA (Non-disclosure Agreement) unless, of course, special circumstances apply.

That said, an NDA is an opportunity to control the extent to which your GD can talk about what they've done—or are doing—for you and your logo design project. You may wish to openly invite as much exposure as possible and love the fact that your GD openly talks about how you are a client of theirs. They may even wish to show the ongoing development of your logo. This may generate welcomed publicity for your brand, as live projects often have a special quality that captures people's imaginations. Alternatively, you may warrant your GD only talks about your logo after it has been completed, or is only allowed to showcase it in their portfolio (online and/or off-) for a limited period. You may even request they make absolutely no mention of it at all. Whatever your preference, the NDA is your opportunity to control how much your GD mentions their professional involvement with you.

## Good graphic design—like many other successful parts of your business—needs good communication

Graphic design is a special place where value can be added by the truckload but it is also a minefield of potential misunderstanding. As with any creative project, the keywords are communication and visibility. As long as you are wisely placed in the review and development process in a way that suits both yourself and the people crafting your identity, your feedback will be used effectively to help—and add value to—the end result.

**Start writing your identity brief. Download the brief template at: giveyourselfabrand.com/id-brief**

## And now relax—but not too much

As long as you've followed the previous steps in this book, have used the brief sheets—available at ***giveyourselfabrand.com/id-brief***—and have chosen a GD you trust, then relax.

Come to a working agreement you are both happy with and let them do the hard work. That's what you're paying them for. Pretty soon, you will be looking at the logo that will identify your brand for years to come, and that's very exciting.

But don't relax too much. When you get your brilliant logo back from your GD, don't make the mistake of thinking your branding work has finished. It has only just begun.

> Logos serve a key role in the branding process but they are not the full picture and are only one aspect of your brand.

A strong consistent identity is an opportunity to gain new fans and build trust among existing ones but the relevance and quality of your foundation, your ACTivity, and that which you can offer the world as a result of this, will be the greatest influencing forces behind your relationships and ultimate success. As Paul Rand said earlier, 'a logo gets its meaning from the quality of the thing it represents, not the other way around.'

---

'A logo is a period at the end of a sentence,
not the sentence itself.'
*Sagi Haviv*

---

## How can I protect my identity?

Once you have produced your primary identity—i.e. your logo, or 'trademark' do you need to protect it? What are the threats?

The threat is two-fold:

- someone may copy your logo or create one very similar to yours, thus confusing your audience and potentially damaging your brand's power to operate
- someone may accuse you of copying their logo and may take legal action against you to prevent you from using your logo.

To best avoid the above two-fold threat:

1). Ensure the mark you create is Distinctive and Unique

2). Establish a meaningful connection—between your brand, the mark, and an audience—as soon as possible. The sooner people start to associate your brand and its key offerings with your brand identity, the sooner your brand identity starts to gain greater value and protection.

As long as your identity is original, distinctive, and unique, it gains protection by virtue of uniqueness and relevance i.e. it becomes relevant to a certain audience of end-users, however, the best way to protect your brand identity is by registering it as a registered trademark. This helps you to:

- enhance your brand's image, credibility, and authority as it shows you are a serious player people can trust.
- secure exclusivity of use.*

If you wish to apply to get your logo registered—as a registered trademark, so it can carry the ® symbol—you will need to contact the relevant agent or authority in your territory. In the UK, such an application can be made through the HMRC website:

Visit www.gov.uk and search for 'Apply to register a trademark'.

* i.e. only your brand can use this trade name and trademark and enables you a very strong legal position to both protect your brand from any infringement claims and to prevent and deter other brands from misappropriating—or infringing on—your identity, IP, trademark, and goodwill.

Meanwhile, it can be worth adding a 'TM' symbol to your logo to show the world that this is a trademark you claim ownership of and use—however, it does not really carry any real additional legal protection.

---

'There are three responses to a piece of design—yes, no, and WOW! Wow is the one to aim for.'

*Milton Glaser, designer of the original I ♥NY logo*

---

**Run a RUDE check on your logo options by downloading the worksheet at: giveyourselfabrand.com/ checkyouridentity**

**STEP 7**

# Give your brand a style

What are you like?

## What is a style and why do you need one?

Let's just take a minute to reflect that you've made it to here.

Wow.

Everything is starting to come together. You've now got—or soon have—an identity ... which is a MAJOR turning point and a truly EPIC layer of your brand's foundation.

So what's next?

Well, now we take everything we've done, and continue to work it all up, with the momentum we have from your new identity, and we develop your style, a wider and fuller expression of your brand.

'Style' is an organising principle that guides a brand's many disparate Touchpoints into one identifiable collective.

Like your ethos, style is another golden thread that pulls everything together but in a tangible way that others can appreciate.

Your style can be simple or complex; set down and prescribed into a "Style Bible" or governed wordlessly via its makers and shakers. It can be bold and obvious or it can be subtle and hard-to-put-your-finger-on. But no matter what your style is, it should always be distinctive, authentic, persistent, pervasive, expressive, and relevant. And it should say, in some way: 'Here is yet another manifestation of our inimitable brand.'

Style is the way in which you shape the substance of your brand's offerings and touchpoints into a tangible means of expression and identity.

'Puh!' scoffs Uncle Brian, shaking his head while eating some cereal, 'style sounds like a load of frilly nonsense!'

Well, Brian, maybe. Maybe when style is all there is, when it's all froth and no coffee, all mouth and no trousers, just hot air, and illusion, without any core value or substance,* then sure, style alone can become trite, tasteless, and adrift.

However, when a brand uses its style to fully express itself in—and impress itself on—the world, your style becomes the key that unlocks greater brand recognition and leverage.

Which is very powerful for a brand.

So, shut up, Brian. And make sure you wash that bowl.

* People often lecture on the importance of 'substance' (over style) but ironically the word 'substance' itself concedes that substance sits below (or 'sub') the 'stance' i.e. the style. (I may have had too much Cheekipop.)

Style can enable every aspect of your brand to become greater than the sum of its parts.

We all appreciate style is a tangible expression of identity and values.

Compare your most favourite music with your least favourite music. In terms of substance, they are probably both very similar—the songs you love share a great deal of substance with songs you hate: the same underlying science, the same structures. Both use beats and bridges and vocals and notes. An F sharp here, a C minor there—and yet one gives you joy and the other despair. Why? What makes all the difference?

The answer, Brian, is style.

The details, the choices, the flourishes that make all the difference. Why do people love a certain film? Why do they love a certain shirt, car, holiday destination, or restaurant dish?

It is because of style.

The choices that have been made.

The choices in the particular cut of a dress, that fabric, that colour. The choice to use that actor, that herb, that varnish, material, or time signature. The choice Jeep made to use round headlights, the choice Quentin Tarantino made to cast John Travolta, the choice Adele or Otis Redding made to go up a note at just the right moment. The detail that makes you notice. The choice that wins the day. The flourish that captures the heart.

Style is a brand's unique relationships to materials, words, pictures, sounds, and touch. And we humans—the social, sensuous, style-conscious tribal beings that we are—love it or hate it, however, it is conveyed.

The sweeping aerial footage at the start of a high-budget thriller, the turn of a model's head, the lift of an actor's eyebrow, the sound of the car door, the weight of the keyfob, the comedian's ( ... ) pause, the choice of thread in the upholstery, the use of tangerine and turquoise in the carpet pattern.

Everything is a balance between style and substance.

We all communicate through style. Style gets measured.

Style helps you communicate and express.

It doesn't mean you have to be "stylish" or vain, or sport only the latest high street trend, it just means the authentic style that you use to express your brand's personality to its audience. And as a brand, you only exist to your audience across the touchpoints where it encounters you.

For any touchpoint to be successful its audience needs to ORATE it. A well-defined and expressed style helps a brand's touchpoints get Observed, Realised as being relevant, Aspired towards, Trusted and Engaged with.

As your brand's style is simply a wider and fuller expression of its primary identity, it must first be recognised by the end-user as a thing that belongs to your brand. This doesn't mean you have to put your logo on every available surface—that could be counter-productive, as people quickly get cheesed off when overexposed to a highly repetitive piece of information—but you must ensure your end-user knows they are dealing with your brand, otherwise, it's wasted effort.

Branding is about ownership. So, own your style.

It's a good idea to look at the end-user's journey in any particular scenario to see where they are most likely to interact with your touchpoints. Always look at the context of the situation to see how you can communicate your brand's inimitable style using intelligence and subtlety. Style helps your touchpoints get ORATE'd but it also helps to build up a greater picture of what your brand is to its audience. It shows people who you are. It creates a world. A world of trust and inspiration.

Style is any convention you have the imagination, means, and confidence to pull off. This could be the wearing of a funky wide-brimmed hat, the use of magenta, or the decision to use no hyphenation in your books at the line ends.

Your brand is to be an ongoing process and over its life, your brand's style is going to be communicated via countless touchpoints. And you cannot be expected to know the form and function of every touchpoint.

But you don't have to.

All you need do now is set the mood.

Lay down the "keynotes". Lay down just enough information to set the mood and describe the tune. The basic yet distinctive tune that is unique to your brand. Just enough beats to suggest the rhythm.

You just need to decide upon a few touchpoints that encapsulate and communicate a suggestion of your brand's style, personality, and substance.

Reveal a teasing glimpse of what is to come.

You can lock down as little or as much as you want at this stage. Whatever touchpoints you wish to create are up to you but please do refer to the GYAB Touchpoint checklist for guided inspiration available to download at ***giveyourselfabrand.com/touchpoint-tactics***

Now you have the founding mission principles of your why and ethos, now that you have a better idea of who it is you are to serve, what you're to be called, and how you're to be identified, now is the time to give your brand a style.

---

'Fashion is what you buy,
style is what you do with it.'
*Nicky Hilton*

---

## Style takes many forms

The opportunities to express your brand's style are almost infinite. However, no matter what your touchpoints happen to be, your brand will most likely be operating on planet Earth and communicating with humans, using the impressive systems and technologies we have already established for the sharing of ideas. These agreed-upon paradigms include colour, language, art, music, fashion, and Morris dancing.

We communicate with one another and touch each other via posters, spoken words, hand gestures, chitchat, text messages, radio adverts, filmed scenes, handshakes, applause, opera, banter, whiteboards, and writing names on coffee cups with black marker pens. We communicate via the style of our haircuts, the cut of our hemlines, the way we uncap bottles, the sound of our motorbikes, the quality of our biscuits, and the posture we adopt to drink wine at parties.

As a brand, it's your job to decide which touchpoint opportunities—and methods of communication—will serve you best. I will talk more about how to better communicate in the voice chapter (next chapter) but meanwhile, to help you make better decisions about how to find and express your brand's style, I will now list some valuable "rules of thumb". Stand clear.

## A good style should be DAPPER

From the outset of your brand-building you will have opportunities to develop and express your brand's style, and at each juncture, your style should be **D.A.P.P.E.R.** It should be:

**Distinctive**

**Authentic**

**Persistent**

**Pervasive**

**Expressive**

**Relevant**

Can your style be truthfully described by these six key adjectives?

### Is your style Distinctive?

If you see a paragraph of black text and one word is **different** which word will you look at first? The different one i.e. distinctive one. The one that stands out.

It's an evolutionary thing, our minds evolved to look for odd things that stand out of the picture. When we are confronted with a piece of information we immediately start defining the context and the rules, to ask 'What does this information mean?'

Things that stand out get our attention.

Sometimes, that can be a drawback.

If you're trying to evade a sniper (or comments from a comedian) it's not a great idea to stand out, but in branding, it can be very valuable, so lean into it.

If your brand's style is the same as many other brands, why would people notice or use yours over another one? Does your brand stand out? Can people identify your brand from a rival brand?

Your brand needs to be noticed, by certain people, by your audience, to grow and flourish. The keyword is 'distinctive' not 'infamous' so beware of how you get noticed—but your brand's style should be perceptible enough to be noticed. What are your audiences going to recognise about your brand? If it's true that your brand is 'what people say it is, when you leave the room', then much of that relates to—and can be influenced by—your brand's style. That is to say, the distinctive manifestation of its underlying core. What would you like to hear if you eavesdropped?

## Is your style Authentic?

Authenticity is simply the confident expression of one's beliefs. You can usually tell when someone or something is being authentic.

Ability + Desire + Courage = Confidence.

Confidence is from the Latin 'con' for 'with' and 'fidere' meaning 'to trust' and 'have faith'. Confidence = 'with faith'.

It comes from actually listening to your motivational muses, it comes from giving yourself permission and it comes from having had the patience to earn that confidence.

Often you know something is authentic before you can process why. We have more trust in authentic things.

When we believe we can do something, we are confident in doing it and that comes across and creates authenticity. If we try to do something we don't believe we can do, then we're not confident in doing it, and so we then appear inauthentic. Others pick up on that quite quickly. It's why inexperienced comedians often fail to win over a crowd, or why we'd likely feel self-conscious, and likely blush, going to work in a full-body gimp suit.*

Humans can usually size things up in about two seconds, and they know when someone isn't quite being an authentic version of themselves. Confidence is something we can judge and perceive so innately that we can almost sense it. A baby will quickly let the room know if the hands she's in don't feel confident.

---

'You create a credible brand by staying true
to who you are.'
*Hillary Sawchuk*

---

* Although to be fair, if there's one outfit sure to mask your blushes it's a fully-body gimp suit.

If you believe you can do something, you're halfway there. The athlete who knows she can win the race often wins the race and the ones who aren't as sure, usually don't.

Whatever Abilities, Content, or Touchpoints your brand engages in—or uses—to ACT out your brand, the first question should be, 'Is this an authentic expression?'

If you ask this question, your brand's style will take care of itself. Your budgets will go further and your audience will be attracted, enlarged, retained, and delighted.

Your brand could be a leather-clad gang of motorcycling priests called The Holy Rollers. As long as you have the blessing of your bishop—why *not* spread the word on customised Harley-Davidsons? No trade or industry sector has a monopoly on authenticity. You can be an authentic florist, an authentic civil engineering business, or an authentic hen nite organiser.

There's no law to say hen nite organisers can't use PowerPoint presentations and scaled models—and why can't civil engineering companies use karaoke bars or inflatable hats? (Although it's probably sensible for architects to avoid using edible penises.)

When you are being authentic, you are making sense because you are being real and you have an integrity that you own, that no one can copy or steal. Authenticity inspires Trust, and Trust inspires Engagement.

## Is your style Persistent and Pervasive?

Consistent branding is good branding and style is a huge part of branding, so it pays to be persistent and pervasive with whatever style elements you decide to introduce and present. By that I mean you need the distinctive features of your style to reach every part of your brand and maintain a long-term presence.

"Global roll-outs" of style over long-term campaigns will help you ensure consistency across your brand, compound the impact of your style-based decisions, reduce confusion, and build trust.

And when I say "global" I mean you must have a style that is pervasive right around, and throughout, the "world of your brand"—not necessarily around the whole of Planet Earth. If you're a part-time dog walker, limited to one postcode, "global roll-out" would mean applying your persistent style across all your relevant touchpoints. For example, your business cards, website, bumper stickers, and branded doggie coats. These items should share common details and characteristics.

Create a global style that expresses the foundation of who your brand is no matter where you're touching your audience, whether that's in London, Paris, New York, Tokyo, Weston-super-Mare, or a small town in Germany.

By persistent I mean, keep at it and honour your style over the long term. If you chop and change your "look-and-feel" every five minutes, you may confuse your audience and weaken your brand's potency. easyJet rolled out its distinctive and simple brand style—mostly orange—in 1995 and has kept it ever since. It didn't roll out a new typeface, or different colours or throw in any dramatic new style feature out of boredom or fear of getting stale. Instead, it has introduced continuous improvements and details to its offerings and Touchpoints and has stayed up-to-date in hundreds of important ways, but ultimately it has stayed faithful to its identity and style. This goes a very long way in building trust and brand equity. As a result, easyJet is now not only a very distinctive brand but also a very strong and trusted one.

Style can work very effectively if it's simple, obvious, and tightly defined because people like things they can rely on in a fast-moving and ever-changing world. However, your style needn't be simple, obvious, and tightly defined—because people are also intelligent and sophisticated and love nuance and change. It's up to you to think about your unique brand and how its offering will best be conveyed to its audience but ultimately, when it comes to a brand's style: Persistence and Pervasiveness are two very precious 'P's indeed.

> You need not roll out something "globally" all in one go. It's often a good idea to test something before you commit to it, just in case it's flawed or incomplete. Tests and gentle "phase-ins" such as 'soft launches' or 'A/B Tests' provide a means to study—and experiment with—your style considerations before you fully commit to them. Testing certain style elements at the start of, or throughout, your ongoing brand-building can be done by giving yourself a 'Style Trial'. (Jump forward two pages.)

## Is your style Expressive and Relevant?

Your style cannot help but be Expressive. Anything that exists, expresses meaning to an audience, whether it is aware of it or not. The red carpet expresses "high status" to the gathered throngs and the injured antelope expresses "easy lunch" to the leopard.

To express is to cause a reaction.

So, always ask yourself, 'Is my style causing the right reactions in the minds and hearts of my intended audience?'

'How does my style express my brand's reason-for-being?'

'How does my style express my values?'

'What exactly is my style expressing? And where?'

Because whatever it is, it should be Relevant. Showing how your brand is relevant is vital so your end-users can ORATE. Style influences and determines the form and function of all of your brand's Touchpoints. It regulates the surface presentation of everything your audience of end-users interacts with, so your audience needs to recognise and appreciate your style.

Your style has got to make sense to your audience.

You can be as conformist or "off-the-wall" as you want, as long as your audience is right there with you, identifying with you and reacting to you, understanding and valuing, or even questioning, what it is you are doing.

If you lose your audience, through "irrelevant" expressions, you need to get it back quickly. Discordance can shake things up and create space for wonder and discovery, but if you don't give a resolution to the discord, people will be left confused and may leave.

Your style is an opportunity to connect.

---

'It's not about brand,
it's about style.'
*Anon*

---

## Give yourself a Style Trial

A "Style Trial" can take many forms but ultimately it's just an opportunity for your brand to test things out, before you commit to them and before you go public with your expressions. A chance to use, modify, delete, or retain certain features and styles across your touchpoints before you—

'Ok, I get it,' sniffs Uncle Brian, stooped over the sink, 'but how would I give myself a "Style Trial" if for example, I was a Sheet Metal Merchant, what exactly would I put on trial?'

Well, first, Brian, you'd need to consider which touchpoints would best serve you. I'm no expert in the steel trade but as a rough starting point I might suggest the following touchpoint areas that could bring value to your company's brand:

> adverts, videos, websites, emails—ebooks and other downloadable resources you could use for engagement or as teaser items to give away in exchange for the email addresses you will need to capture (with permission) to build your list and send your emails to—printed literature, product demonstrations, uniform, caps, t-shirts, livery, van vinyls, merchandise, stationery, interior design, banners for expo events and trade fairs, gizmos, widgets and posts on social media platforms.

All these things are opportunities to convey your brand's DAPPER style. Each one in isolation is not that exciting (like all the things that make up a party, remember? Drinks, pork pies, Malcolm and Sue from next door) but when they come together: boom! Your style starts to party. And the bigger the party—between you and your audience of end-users—the better for everyone, and the more successful your brand becomes.

A Style Trial can show you a preview or 'taster' before you commit to any style considerations. You can trial colours, imagery, fabrics, and fonts, and look at them applied to sample touchpoints like websites, merchandise, packaging, literature, or inflatable dinosaurs. A Style Trial can be very valuable when you're thinking about the wider expression of your brand identity beyond the logo i.e. your Style.

It's a great way to trial and review ideas before full commitment. And can include samples, and swatches, to give you options on available and appropriate colours and fabrics, materials, typefaces, equipment, and any necessary visual consideration. It can include artist's visuals, a mood board, a 3D computer-generated "fly-through"—anything to make your Touchpoints come alive and help you visualise.

A good GD or GD Agency or Project Manager—working with the necessary suppliers—should be able to put together enough of a Style Trial to help you taste and test out all options before commitment. However, you can do a lot of trialling by yourself. Especially if yours is a personal brand. By pulling together references and sourcing ideas and materials, you can start to see what works and record a colourful palette of options. Give yourself time to make accidents, as they often bear the most fruit. But get it done and have fun.

## Give yourself a Style Bible

Once you've defined—and committed to—your particular style decisions, it can then be good practice to create a "Style Bible" of some form. For many brands, this usually takes the form of a definitive set of brand guidelines (or 'brand standards', 'brand manual', 'brand book', 'style guide', 'toolkit', etc.). Creating such a rulebook lets you define your brand's visual system—your colours and typefaces, your menus and uniforms—the laws of your style.

These are usually confidential documents created for 'controlled sharing' among internal audiences—such as in-house staff, brand partners, and appointed agencies—but they can also be shared in the public domain. Brands such as Instagram and X (formerly Twitter) have downloadable toolkits for their users. Such widespread partnering is not suitable for all brands and it is good to retain certain controls over your touchpoints—however as brands begin to see more value in atomising their offerings over an ever-growing variety of engagement platforms, it is always wise to consider which parts you need to control and which parts you could afford to outsource or "democratise".

However you wish to share your Style Bible, having one available ensures the unique visual system of your brand gets authentically reproduced across all touchpoints. Especially valuable if your brand's touchpoints are being created by disparate designers and suppliers.

The level of detail you define and document is up to you and the time and expense you apportion for such a document will depend on your needs. In my years of using and designing such Style Bibles, I have seen a variety of approaches varying in length, density, and detail. I've seen documents five pages long, and 200 pages long. I have seen intranets and websites with training videos. I have seen professionally printed manuals that look like glossy Annual Reports and I've seen tea-stained dog-eared sheets roll-bound together. These days, it usually takes the form of a pdf.

> It's a good idea to create a skeleton version that outlines the items you'd like to cover—structured by chapter—and then add and embellish where necessary (see example overleaf).

You can devote chapters to your brand's "founding fathers", your social responsibility work, or your abiding relationship with Yorkshire. You can use words like "mission", "vision", "essence", 'history', 'back story', 'tomato' and 'supernova'—but chances are, most people who use the guidelines will probably just skip through to the necessary typeface information and/or colour breakdowns. But when it comes to creating your brand's Style Bible, there is always value in doing more rather than doing less, as it's easier for a reader to flick past an irrelevant page than to flick to a page that's not there. But you don't want—or need—to add any "filler" material. You shouldn't be adding "filler" material to any Content you produce, but it's especially dumb doing it for a Style Bible, as its two key roles are to:

A). Act as an inspirational touchstone for a trusted, usually internal, audience.
B). To provide a rulebook that ensures your brand is reproduced authentically no matter who is reproducing it or where it is being reproduced.

You probably do not have time to employ "enforcers" or "Brand Police" so a Style Bible does the job of making things official and ensuring all identifying marks and features—such as logos, colour palettes, and typographical rules—are correctly reproduced, in the right way, with the right colours and the right fonts, and in the right pattern using the correct layout.

In the early stages of your brand building, it helps to do this work in stages and treat the Style Bible as a "living document" that can grow. However, as a basic structure, you might want to consider something like this:

- Introduction / Overview
- Our Values
- Assets (showing what the brand assets are and how to handle them)
    - Identity/Logo (clear space, minimum size, positioning re. other elements)
    - Typography (the font family and hierarchy for print and digital use)
    - Colour (primary and secondary palettes)
    - Use of submarks, straplines, and other graphical devices designed to work alongside the primary logo as part of the brand's overall visual system
- Photography (examples of appropriate images, plus DOs and DON'Ts)
- Grids (Layout guidelines to help designers recreate branded content)
- Tone-of-Voice* (as brands find themselves outsourcing more and more content, with the rise of social media, many brand guidelines now include Tone-of-Voice recommendations such as 'words we use and words we don't use')
- Examples of the brand in action (i.e. a Style Trial, with visuals across various Touchpoints e.g. printed and digital media, dummy adverts, brochure covers, headlines, billboards, wireframes, clothing, signage, livery, and other scenarios depending on the nature of the brand)
- Further info/useful links (usually containing links to downloadable templates, artwork assets, and further guidelines).

Having such a document available, comprehensive yet succinct, provides the necessary suppliers and associates—such as creative directors, planners, art directors, graphic designers, photographers, copywriters, and PR and marketing specialists—with a recipe book so they can authentically recreate your brand no matter where they are.

* In the voice section (STEP 8), I do make a reasoned challenge to this widely-use term 'Tone-of-voice' but, despite being a slightly confused and blinkered term, it is widely-used so no harm for now in retaining it here.

## Colour

As we saw when looking at your identity, colours are important—and intelligent use of colour can add great value to your brand—however, it's important to choose well and set down style rules for how your brand handles colour.

This can be set down in your Style Bible.

Opting for a brand palette of one strong colour or one strong colour pair and combining them with the supporting "accent" colours of a secondary palette—featuring whites, blacks, greys, and complementary colours—is a good practice. For example, your brand's primary palette—which is often decided during the creation of a brand's primary identity—may feature a strong pair of colours that make up the brand's "primary palette". As previously mentioned a successful primary palette is usually best limited to just one or two (sometimes more) colours—e.g. easyJet's orange and white—however it can also be very useful to complement this "hero palette" with a secondary palette of 'accent' or 'complementary' colours, for sub-branding, colour-coding or just to add interest.

For example, your primary colour palette may 'Azure Blue' and 'Neon Peach'.

This pairing could then be supported by the use of white, black, grey, and perhaps even the use of a third 'accent' colour ('Victorian Skies' maybe?) presented as a device like a distinctive 'silver ribbon' if you'd prefer.

However, if you start adding other strong colours to this primary palette they may dilute and confuse the palette. Remember what I said about how adding colours can lessen brand potency?

If for example—you chuck in a 'Swamp Fever' and/or a 'Champagne Beige'—you could easily start to dilute your brand's visual identity and confuse your audience. So good practice is to include a secondary palette along with rules. These "serving suggestions" can then guide designers as to the advised usage of these supporting colours. For example, you may impose a rule that states, 'if using Swamp Fever, use it ONLY as a complementary colour to 'Azure Blue' and any usage should not exceed 25% of the overall usage of 'Azure Blue', i.e. there should always be a ratio of four parts 'Azure Blue' to one part 'Swamp Fever'. You can also lay down rules for tints of colours, and gradients.

You can tell stories through colour. You can build up a palette that creates a strong narrative—and a DAPPER style—but do consider the hierarchies and proportions of usage, because these subtle rulings on how you use the colours do make a big difference overall.

---

'Simplicity is the ultimate sophistication.'
*Leonardo da Vinci*

---

'Simple can be harder than complex: You have to work hard to get your thinking clean to make it simple.'
*Steve Jobs*

---

## Supporting typefaces a.k.a. other fonts

The core elements of a brand's identity should be fixed into place from Day One (that is to say between choosing your name and developing your style). However, when you start doing business in the real world you might naturally encounter new challenges and opportunities that require extending your brand's identity. As your brand wins new ground and covers an ever-growing "Terrain of Touchpoints"—you may find new ways to apply your brand and express its style. Without a crystal ball, it can be difficult to foresee every bridge you'll need to cross. However, one common thing that trips up a brand owner following the completion of their primary identity is additional typefaces, or as they are more commonly known: other fonts.

In the design and development of your brand identity, you are either about to or are currently, looking at the best typefaces for your primary logo. (If you have already created your primary logo, congratulations.) However, do not overlook the selection of your brand's secondary, or tertiary, font that will complement your identity.

You may have done this already as part of your identity creation, especially if you are creating versions of your primary identity featuring your strapline.

A brand's strapline—i.e. line—is usually reproduced in its 'secondary typeface'.

Whatever other fonts you have chosen for your brand, it is good practice to put rules in place and establish certain hierarchies for your brand's chosen palette of fonts, to ensure authentic and consistent reproduction across all necessary touchpoints.

It's also valuable to assign other rules around these other fonts, such as preferred font sets for digital reproduction—websites, apps, etc. Much of this can be finessed with time, depending on usage requirements, but where possible it is good to define which weights and sizes work for various scenarios, for example for headlines, body copy, etc.

It's also a good idea to include rules around web-based fonts for online use. The functionality and choice of web-based fonts is impressive and has come on a long way in the last few years, however with many online Touchpoints—e.g. email design and email management—the font options can still be quite limited, hence why many brands prudently use a shortlist, or a "hierarchy of preferences" for their rules around web-based fonts i.e. 'where possible use **DIN** but if **DIN** isn't available, use Arial, and if Arial isn't available, use generic Sans-serif.'

## How will you dress your brand?

How can you dress and style your brand?

What will be the colour, form, shape and texture of your Touchpoints?

What equipment will you use/ Which fabrics will go well with each other?

Which touchpoints are you going to think about first?

Digital? Physical? Animal, mineral, or vegetable? Your stationery? Your emails? Your website? Your shop window? Your product prototype? Your pitch, presentation, or proposal? Your exhibition stand? Your engagement widgets? Your seminar? Your webinar? Your VR demo? Your vehicles? Your launch party? Uniforms? Table cloths? Tool belts?

Whether it's your business cards or your backstage passes, your brochures, or your pop-up bagel kitchens, your Touchpoints are all opportunities to dress your brand and convey your DAPPER style.

The touchpoints of an electric bike store will most likely not be the same as those of a copywriting service. However, whether you are a local sheet metal merchant or an international communications agency. You will need to look at your unique brand foundation and offering and look at where you wish to touch your audiences and how you can use, improve, and express your brand's style.

Style will govern how you A.C.T. And should dictate the media that will bridge the connections between your brand and those it is being built to serve. Because serve you must. After all, as Mr Yoshida once said 'No one prospers unless he renders benefits to others.'

Style will help you determine and refine the bridging points, the means of engagement, and the media. But to determine and refine the messages carried by your brand's media you will also need to consider your voice, which we will address in the next chapter.

---

'Style is something each of us already has, all we need to do is find it.'
*Diane von Furstenberg*

---

**Find your brand's style by downloading the worksheet at: giveyourselfabrand.com/findyourstyle**

## STEP 8

# Give your brand a voice

How do you **communicate?**

## What is a voice and why do you need one?

Give yourself a massive fist bump, we have made it to the final step of your foundation-building work and you are now sitting at the helm of a very strong brand that is going to change your life, the lives of others, and the wider world at large.

But, as Lieutenant Columbo says, 'Err, just one more thing.'

And that one more thing is voice.

The eighth, and final step, all about your brand's ability to actively communicate.

Which is important.

Because in life, business, and branding: active communication is key.

So far, you have put together a powerful entity that knows where it's going, how it's getting there, and for whom. And your brand now has—or is about to have—a strong name, identity, strapline, and style.

However, as even the most laconic brand will surely attest, without active communication through an authentic voice*, your brand simply won't function.

You can spend time and money developing an amazing foundation but if your brand finds it has a failure to communicate, all will be lost.

Ultimately, 'voice' is simply: message management.

It's the way your brand chooses to present certain information to the world.

It is your brand's communicational intelligence and persona.

In completing this step—through a few simple exercises, questions, and considerations—you will develop a brand that people want to do business with.

---

'There's power in allowing yourself to be known
and heard, in owning your unique story,
in using your unique voice.'
*Michelle Obama*

---

* Voice is often referred to by professionals as 'Tone-of-voice' but as you will read I believe this statement needs careful handling.

Voice is closely related to style, but more concerned with the Content that fills your Touchpoints rather than the actual physical Touchpoints themselves. A distinctive and authentic voice enhances your brand's personality and your brand's ability to communicate.

> Voice is the character, form, and movement of the message—whereas style is the character, form, and movement of the media.

Voice is the words you use, and how you say them, rather than your choice of visual elements such as fonts, colours, or fabrics.

Obviously, your voice relates to, and ties in with, your style. Your style will influence your voice, and vice versa, but I'd like to underscore the distinction here because I feel it's an important one. And will certainly help you in devising the voice of your brand.

Success in branding, marketing, and communications is about what you know, but it's also about how you present what you know.

Branding is ultimately about identity. And ownership of your identity. And how you express that identity. This ownership and expression of your brand identity is a choice—and a series of choices that you make—which informs you and the wider world exactly who you are, how you see things, and how you say things. This ownership of expression shows what you choose to pay attention to and how you choose to express your brand's views.

'Hang on,' frowns Uncle Brian, 'you said your style should be DAPPER.'

Right, Brian. I did.

'Ok, so does that mean a brand's voice should be DAPPER too?'

Yes. Thank you, Brian. Your brand must have a DAPPER voice.

Now, that doesn't mean a loud voice, a charming voice, or even an audible voice—it just means you need to find ways to "hallmark" your informational delivery.

'Why?'

To create considered consistency.

If you can find a signature way of communicating, you create greater brand potency. Ideally, you want a viewer to see one of your adverts read one of your blogs, or watch one of your videos, and make a mental connection—even if it's subconscious—that says 'This feels familiar.'

Your voice and your messaging choices should be Distinctive, Authentic, Persistent, Pervasive, Expressive, and Relevant too. The golden thread of DAPPERness should run through your communications.

The more DAPPER your voice is, the more it can distinguish your brand's Content and the more it can create meaningful dialogues with its various audiences and the wider world of prospective end-users.

When you add your voice to the other seven steps of your brand's foundation you create a very strong platform on which to build a life of Abilities, Content, and Touchpoints.

One thing I have noticed in the Style Bibles of many brands is the tendency to assert their brand has one distinctive tone-of-voice.

However, I feel this is one of the most misunderstood aspects of branding*, and, a brand can have, and most often should have, more than one tone of voice. I see 'tone' as a subset of 'voice'.

- **Voice** is the unchanging "character" of your brand's communications.

- **Tone** is the changeable shape of your voice, the inflection you wish to apply. Your brand can adjust this when necessary to better suit the nature of what you are talking about and to better produce the emotional tone you wish to convey. Having the ability to change your tone can, in many cases, build rapport with those it is speaking to.†

## Variety is the spice of life

A healthy spectrum in a brand's voice often enhances its ability to connect with its audiences. For example, the sports brand Nike has a very distinct identity, style, and voice. It is pretty much always geared toward personal empowerment however this global brand is also well-known for its versatility of messaging. The tone it uses for top-level advertising campaigns (stark, laconic, and spare, for example, 'Find your greatness') will differ from the tone it uses in social media messages which are usually more conversational and laden with emojis.

* What most actually mean when they say 'tone-of-voice' is not '**tone**-of-voice' but '**character**-of-voice'.

† Of course, the voice of some brands will predominantly suit a certain tone over others. For example, your average investment banking brand will generally adopt a more sober tone of voice for the majority of its communications, however, there's no reason why it cannot occasionally weave contrast and variety into its communications to add interest and value. The best brands vary their tone inside a consistent character.

A brand that builds light and shade into its voice can enjoy greater rapport with its end-users, stakeholders, and shareholders.

It's all about your choices.

Voice is choice.

Choice of subject, choice of words, choice of volume, choice of silence.

The real world—in which your brand operates—is an ever-moving weather system of messaging. We have many words, and our choices show who and what we are.

When you are developing your voice you may use copywriters or choose to do it yourself but you must always ask questions like 'Would my brand say something like this?', 'Would my brand use this word?', 'Does my audience care about this?', or 'Does my end-user know us well enough to get the joke?'

If a brand's voice—and tone—is always DAPPER it will go a long way in connecting with its end-user. Ideally, you want your end-user to read or hear your Content—in complete isolation from your logo, colours, or other distinctive brand elements—and still know they are inside the world of your brand.

Sticking firm to a DAPPER voice helps you present information more effectively, create messages that fit with your style, and land right with the audience.

---

'It ain't whatcha write,
it's the way atcha write it.'
*Jack Kerouac*

---

## Develop a good bedside manner

You want your voice and tone to suit how you want your brand to be perceived by its audience. It's good to think about this as, what I like to call, a Voice-and-Tone profile, or simply a "V&T" for short.

The V of which will be an evergreen character of voice, and the T being the tone of any particular message.

As mentioned above, your V will influence your T, but it's good to keep them separate in some sense and know that your brand's voice can maintain a distinct character yet still enjoy wriggle room for all manner of necessary expression.

Life, and business, are, after all, one long conversation.

How your brand is to converse will largely depend on your value offering and which touchpoint you are using. For example, a key voice-delivering touchpoint an airline can use is the in-flight announcement to its passengers. This is usually given by the pilot himself and remains a major point of communication between brand and audience. It can make all the difference between a happy end-user and an unhappy end-user a.k.a. in many cases: an ex-customer.

The pilot does not need to keep talking the whole flight like some deranged drive-time DJ—they simply need to vocalise a few timely, well-informed vignettes, delivered with calm professionalism, at key moments such as after take-off, before landing, and during turbulence. The mood, wording, and level of humour can vary depending on your brand, for example, British Airways often uses lines such as 'Weather at Heathrow this afternoon is warm and sunny with a slight westerly wind. On behalf of the crew, we wish you a safe onward journey.'

Such a tone is very "on brand" for this particular touchpoint however in other places—e.g. advertising—there can be more leeway for humour such as the brilliant campaign in 2018 featuring Asim Chaudry. See YouTube. BA's character is retained but with a definite shift in tone.

The relationship between a brand and its audience is a special thing and is kept alive by more than just the pricing and the roll-on-roll-off-wham-bam-thank-you-mam functionality of its goods and services.

A brand is more than its offering. A brand is an opportunity to take its Abilities—for example, the skills, hardware, and systems to fly planes between airports—but present that in such a way as to add value and consistent character of voice (with variation in tone).

And a good character inspires positive growth across the board.

Apparently, in the US at least, the more you like your doctor's character, the less likely you are to sue them in cases of error or malpractice. And equally, the more you dislike their bedside manner, the more likely you are to find fault with them and the more unforgiving you'll be in the event of an error.*

We humans are simple creatures. If you're standing at a bar waiting for service and the bartender acknowledges you, you're more likely to wait patiently because you feel noticed and assured of future service, however, if the bartender ignores you, you're more likely to walk out. If you are selling something via an eCommerce platform and your end-user has problems with delivery, make sure you send them communication to show you are looking into the matter.

We just want to be seen, cared for and looked after, and if you can speak our language and assure us or make us laugh—in a good way—then you strengthen our relationship. Anyone who's had a long-term relationship knows the importance of good communication and how badly the day can go after just one misheard word or inconsiderate comment. Use your brand's V&T to ensure your audience is 'kept sweet' by your communicational consideration.

## Can a brand have more than one voice?

How you craft, define, and control your voice is up to you, however, it's a good idea to be conservative where possible. Less is more.

One true voice is powerful.

The more you can distil your V&T palette into one strong and distinctive personality the more authentic your brand becomes, the easier it is to stay consistent and the more people will trust you. 'Don't go changing', as they say. As we grow as individuals we do experiments, and as we learn, we sometimes try things out. We change up our character, but ultimately we come to find that when we fix or 'stick' for a while—that is to say, when we stay consistent in our character—we inspire greater trust from people. When someone exhibits a wide range of personalities we find it hard to trust them, we wonder 'What are they really like?'

* In his book *Blink: The Power of Thinking Without Thinking* (previously mentioned on page 143) Malcolm Gladwell discusses how patients' perceptions of their doctors, particularly their bedside manner, can significantly affect their likelihood of filing lawsuits.

A lean V&T can be valuable.

A brand's Content and communications can express—and are expected to express—a wide range of emotions, and sometimes, even conflicting opinions because life is complicated and paradoxical but they should all be expressed through an inimitable voice in a unique way that reinforces and reflects as much of the brand's identifying characteristics as possible.

Coca-Cola for example has a voice that celebrates togetherness and joy. Cynical Uncle Brian would be the first to sneer at any brand's attempt to attach such sentiments to a commercial product but the fact remains that this attachment underpins all successful selling. As humans, we buy that which aligns with our needs. And our needs, if you recall, range from air to self-actualisation. And so, we buy goods and services that we deem appropriate and that we ORATE, and that we trust will transform us inside our frameworks of identity. If you look at the voices of popular brands you will see each one has a distinct and overarching character to its voice. This voice complements its brand foundation and Abilities, Content, and Touchpoints to create a rich world of meaning. A world that is consistently expressed through its V&T. The most successful brands have at their heart a voice that is obvious but nuanced.

Ben & Jerry's is fun and irreverent but also socially conscious.

Tesla is futuristic and sustainable but also fun.

Dove is luxurious but also inclusive and compassionate.

When you add nuance and balance to your brand you create pleasing contrasts that bring brilliant new experiences and offerings into the world.

This is an aspect of branding that can be applied throughout every part of your work and it is just as relevant in honing your voice and messaging.

Flexibility is power.

Yes, your brand's voice should be distinct and consistent, however, you can, and should, adapt it where necessary to suit its environment.

Read the room. Many brands have more than one audience to consider. For example, you may have audiences in different countries with different cultural protocols and ways of doing things. What is acceptable in one place, may not be so acceptable in another.

Where possible, it's always good to adapt your V&T to suit a particular audience if it will create greater rapport but don't adapt to the point that it warps the character of your brand.

## Think about your different audiences

Imagine a popular high-street donut brand called McLoughlin's and an end-user called Barry.

Barry likes donuts so he visits McLoughlin's after a stressful day at the office. He appreciates the service and goods, but that doesn't mean he overtly appreciates every aspect of the brand.

'Who cares if McLoughlin's uses recycled cardboard in its new range of donut packages?' Not Barry!

Barry wants a donut, not a 2000-word manifesto on how McLoughlin's is doing all it can to meet its carbon reduction targets. Such ACTivity would be wasted on end-users like Barry.

But many of McLoughlin's other audiences (e.g. shareholders) might well be interested in such things—probably more so than the donuts themselves. So think hard about who your different audiences are, and how best to speak to each one. This may often simply be a change in tone, or Touchpoint, rather than a change in voice.

It's best not to change anything too dramatically with your voice. But it's always a good idea to think about every place you use it, and if it's connecting in the right way.

## Communication ain't easy, so always consider how your messaging could fail

We so often just assume people will understand us, so we often fail to think about how we're coming over. We slap each other on the back—and congratulate ourselves on our audience-focused communications—completely unaware our audiences are missing most of what we are saying, or throwing those flyers and maildrops straight in the bin, turning the radio off or switching channels to get away from our blanket announcements.

Good Content creation—and basic communication in general—is challenging but with a little bit of thought, feedback, rewriting, and studied technique, we can get better and create better rapport with those we wish to communicate with.

We humans are conscious, social beings, and we love communicating and we have a rich heritage of doing so. The techniques, resources, and potential we now have for connection are greater than ever before, but despite...

...or perhaps because of...

...the sheer breadth of this potential, constant efforts must be made to ensure the meaning we wish to convey gets conveyed successfully.

Communication barriers face us at every turn.

Much of our communication is limited to defined audiences due to differences in language, technology, and tribal/cultural systems, but even between like-minded colleagues who speak in the same tongue, the potential for error is high. We so often assume our audience will 'get' what we're communicating just because we understand it so well ourselves, and we assume our innate understanding of something will translate naturally ... but it is here I invite you to reflect upon how often we miss the mark.

How often have you reread an email you sent a few days ago and thought, 'Oh, that could have been misread! I didn't mean we all wear latex!'

When we talk we can emphasise certain words, and add tonal clues and facial quirks which we cannot add when writing. And so, often, things can get misinterpreted.

We must learn to communicate better, so we can safely use the broad range of resources at our disposal. As you develop your brand's voice think about the many communicational tools we have to take advantage of: accents, slang, sayings, tones, inflections, intonations, volume, pauses (...) crescendos, diminuendos, gestures, eyebrows, scowls, smiles, frowns, ironic expressions of aloofness, exaggeration, understatement, sarcasm, dance, slow-motion, special effects, sound effects, soundtracks, emojis, animated graphics, smoke machines, and montage sequences. Think deeply about how these tools and techniques can be best used, and what the pitfalls might be in using them.

Certain messages are better suited to certain media ... people carry different metrics and meanings with them ... a lot of emphasis and emotion is simply lost in the written word ... television rarely captures atmosphere ... written words rarely convey sarcasm ... jokes often fall flat ... and people rarely care what you did last night. You can deliver the same information a second time with subtle differences and completely change the meaning. Over an audio broadcast, one misheard word can change everything. I spent most of my life thinking Prince was singing about a 'Raspberry *Parade*'.*

If your audience doesn't properly see, hear, or understand your message, or very much care for your views, choice of words, or manner of presentation, or see it as any different from any number of other options, you have a problem.

## Choose well your words

A good Voice-and-Tone—or V&T—is mostly thought about as the spoken voice but the spoken voice is only one form of many message delivery mechanisms.

> Voice is not limited to just what you hear or speak, it can be conveyed across all the senses, across any communicational media.

A good V&T is something the novelist is always striving for. That distinct personality of voice will keep a character fresh, exciting yet relatable, and consistent over three hundred pages. 'Voice' is also relevant and important in moving imagery, graphical communication, literature, stationery, and interactive digital media. Just ask any artist, filmmaker, web designer, or exhibition curator. Anywhere messages are being delivered between a communicator and an audience, you have a V&T framing the message, adding meaning and direction. Most communication—whatever the media—is started by word-based thoughts, because words are often the tools we use to organise our ideas. So word choice is always important. Choose them well.

When he was writing his speeches, Winston Churchill took great care of the words he used. He used Anglo-Saxon words. Short. Direct. Trusted. Words that conjured the right imagery. Imagery that went right to the heart. Language is propaganda. Word choice is key. If you see a

* It's actually 'Raspberry Bidet', of course.

news story saying a 'family' had to 'take refuge' in a 'house' to 'keep warm' you side with them, you want to hug them. But if you see a story about the same event that said the 'home' was 'burglarised' by a 'gang' for 'their own profit', you want to punish them. The same event but different viewpoints with different words trigger different emotions.

## Give yourself Voice-and-Tone guidelines or a V&T 'toolkit' or 'template library'

If you want to create effective Content and communication: get your ideas organised. Choose your words, choose your media, and then storehouse it all. Essentially, start to build up a V&T toolkit. 'Coin' all wording (phrases and language use) that works well into one referable place. Develop your brand's Voice-and-Tone 'guidelines'—or 'template library'—so you can 'clone' things whenever necessary. When you create communications that work, record them. That way you will help give your brand a strong voice that can be consistently delivered.

Branding is a relatively passive discipline in the sense that it does most of its work on itself on its own time before it intrudes into the lives of others, but when you've built your foundation, your platforms, and your subscription lists, it's important to be an active voice in the world. If you don't speak up for your brand, who will?

Developing, defining, and documenting a DAPPER voice helps you tell better stories and capture the imaginations of your end-users. You'll be able to start strong from the gate, from the get-go, with authority, continuity, consistency, empathy, and confidence.

It's worth getting right because your voice influences how your audiences perceive your brand.

Whether you work alone or as part of a team, a V&T Toolkit will help you retain the best of your communications and maintain consistency at all times. Communicating in a branded and uniform manner to any audience is powerful and ensures brand equity. Such a toolkit (or 'house style', if you prefer) is especially valuable if various contributors are aiming to achieve one voice. Such collaborative thinking has always been found in editorial departments of newspapers and magazines but is now a very important aspect of the most successful brands.

> Creating a DAPPER voice full of interest and distinction, expressed as one recognisable character is not easy. But it is something to aim for.

The most effective way to ensure your brand V&T is authentically reproduced in such a way is to use a set of guidelines or a template library, where templates and scripts can be stored and shared. These documents can be used to store and reproduce—i.e. 'coin-and-clone'. Such a storehouse can help people follow tried-and-tested protocols, ask the right questions, at the right time, and do so in a consistent manner. It is a good idea to assign a trusted administrator to 'police' the system, and vet and filter all submissions to ensure the best templates and scripts are made available, under helpful categories, in the formats necessary.

A V&T template library can contain sales scripts, email templates, 'canned responses', guidelines, and anything you'd like coined or minted or 'cookie cut' so any associates, admins, or affiliates can create communications that speak for your brand in its unique yet DAPPER way.

Guidelines are useful for contributor writers or social media aides. And now, with the rise of podcasts, there is a growing use of script-based adverts—where the podcast's host will personally read the advert from a script.

A tight overview of your brand's voice—presented along with a V&T 'toolkit' or 'template library'—gives your brand and its contributors everything everyone needs to produce disparate Content that speaks in one DAPPER voice.

It is good practice to house your V&T toolkit on a cloud-based platform so you can access templates, scripts, and valuable files and templates no matter where you are. Services such as GoogleApps, Dropbox, and Office 365 OneDrive allow you to create such a system and set up 'access privileges' for users. It is good practice to keep a centralised, definitive, and updated version of your V&T toolkit to keep on top of new contributions and amends, however, it is also good practice to 'back-up' frequently, to ensure you have a failsafe version, just in case of malicious or accidental deletion or loss of files. It is also good to employ regular housekeeping and to be mindful of GDPR requirements where data is involved.

## How do I start to give my brand a voice?

I left this stage to the end because...

...even though every step from Name will be tangible to your audience, the subject of developing and defining your **Voice** is a great bridging point between the foundation-building work and the work of Abilities, Content, and Touchpoints that await you.

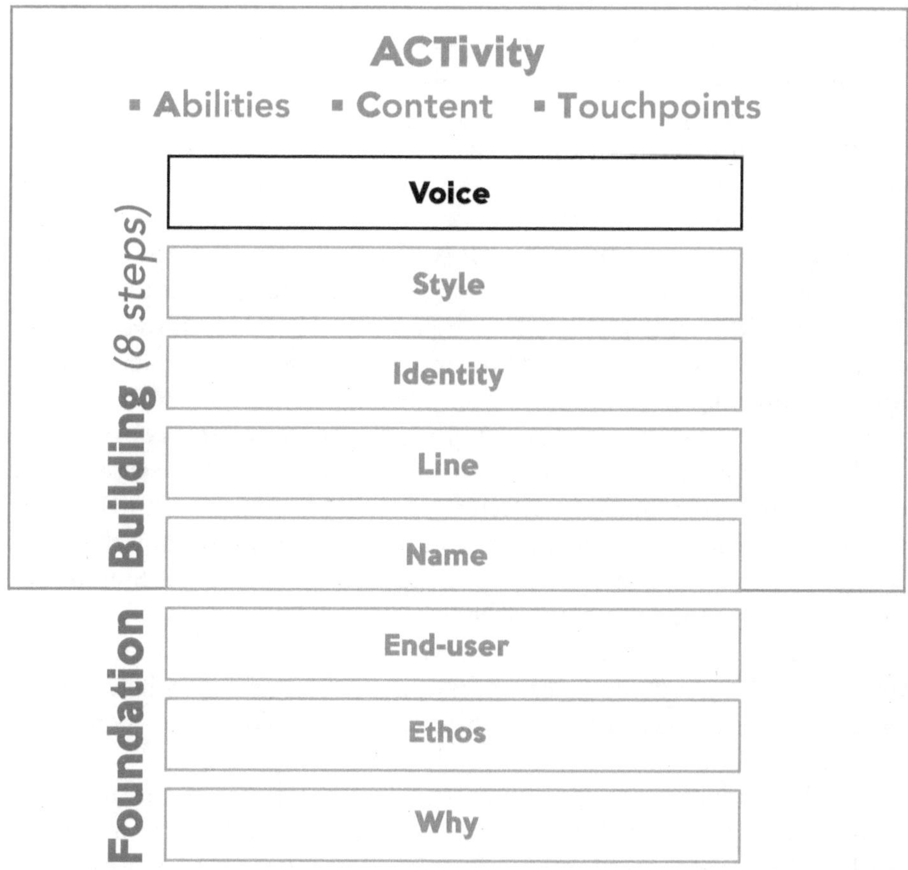


...so now is the time to start thinking well about how you will communicate with your audiences, based on what you've come to discover your brand is as a communicational personality.

When you go to a party and see someone, you can usually assume a lot about them from their appearance alone: like their appearance, hairstyle, fashion sense, height, shoes, etc. ... but until they start communicating, you don't really have a clue about their personality.

It's the same with a *brand's* personality.

People may like your style, but it's the voice that seals the deal. Not necessarily the sound of it (although that can help) but more so the way you choose to use it. What you choose to comment on, and how. Many relationships have been shut down early after an opening conversation.

When you start to create Content and messaging for your brand, start as you mean to go on. Consistency and authenticity are your friends. As we saw with style, you don't have to work out every last detail of your V&T right now—developing an authentic voice is an ongoing and organic process, which often cannot be fully realised and worked out in one go at the very beginning. However, the more you can work out your voice at the very beginning, the better. The trick is to create a forgiving V&T with plenty of wriggle room. Be prescriptive but not overly prescriptive. As the best flower arrangers say 'always leave room for the butterflies'.

Start as you mean to go on. If you propose an overly-contrived or 'high-maintenance' voice such as a declaration to only use the most poetic highfalutin language written by the most sought-after copywriters or to speak only in brilliant witticisms, and use nothing but rhythmic wordplay or sizzling soundbites you may run into trouble. Soundbites are great, sure, they sell—we all love a short-back-and-sides and a Big Mac Meal and knickers with cling-and-ping but sizzling soundbites—like any really good copy—can take time to find and thus be costly to produce. Good copywriting is a fine art. And takes time. Writing is rewriting.

The best advice is to root your brand's voice in the truth of who it really is as a character. Who it is speaking to, and what its foundational truth is. Essentially, all the things you've just defined through the eight steps of the GYAB brand-building process. If your brand's voice is rooted in the truth of this foundation, it will stand out and attract and engage and retain the authentic audience it was created to serve and it will ring true with every word and every message, every video, email, press release, TED talk and training conference.

Choosing what to say or what to present—and choosing which Touchpoint to present it through—will become a constant consideration throughout your brand-building and Content creation. No matter what you're creating—the signs in your shop windows, the stories on your product labels, the titles on your website, the phrases in your podcasts—if you have taken the time to think about your brand's voice, and you do the work of pulling together ideas, guidelines and resources to aid your mode and process of presentation, your communication will come over as more professional, considered, authentic and enjoyable.

---

'The only way to find your voice is to use it.
It's hardwired, built into you.
Talk about the things you love.
Your voice will follow.'
*Austin Kleon*

---

**Find your brand's voice by downloading the worksheet at: giveyourselfabrand.com/findyourvoice**

# Part 4

# Give your brand a review

Before we crack open the champagne and rush out the door to kiss a stranger, let's just make a few final checks.

**Consolidate and review your brand's foundation in one place by downloading the worksheet at: giveyourselfabrand.com/brandreview**

# Part 5

# And now it's time to A.C.T.

## Remember: people don't want your brand, *they want what your brand can do for them*

Firstly, well done. You've completed the eight-step foundation-building process, which means you now have a brand, and can now begin to give your brand a life. A life of Abilities, Content, and Touchpoints.

A life of ACTivity (oh yeah, this stuff writes itself.)

But before we get too excited, let's just remind ourselves that people don't really want your brand, they only really want what your brand can do for them. As we saw earlier, your end-user, or potential end-user has just one question, 'What's in it for me?' Or rather, 'How can you transform me?'

Everything in life is just the transformation of energy, and it's always been that way, ever since the Big Bang, some 13.8 billion years ago. But then one day, social, conscious beings came along and started living together and growing together and having thoughts and sharing them using ideas to communicate and promote peaceful coexistence. And naturally, branding grew out of that process. And then you found this book and worked through the eight steps to create a solid foundation on which to build your brand. This means now, you can A.C.T. Now you can perform!

'Right,' sniffs Uncle Brian, 'but perform what? Can't we just go and get my business cards printed?'

Patience, Brian. Patience. Before we throw the launch party, let's just take one last lesson on how we can use this eight-step foundational platform to move forward and create a wonderful world of Abilities, Content, and Touchpoints.

---

'The biggest part of leadership is that you lead by example with your performance first and foremost.'
*Jude Bellingham*

---

## It's time to think about your future performances, it's time to A.C.T.

Are you ready to A.C.T.? Are you ready to get ACTive? The answer is 'yes' by the way. Yes, you are ready. We could get business cards printed now because we have the brand name, line, identity, style, and voice locked in. And we know why you're starting this brand, how it will conduct itself, and who it will do that for. Yes, you have a solid foundation on which to give your brand a life of ACTivity. But let's just remind ourselves what A.C.T. stands for...

***A is for Abilities. And these are what your brand can do***; your Abilities inform the primary business of your brand. For example, if you're a tax consultancy brand, it is because you—or someone on your behalf who can work within your brand—can advise people on their tax issues. If you're a hotel brand it is because you and your team can provide people with accommodation. You may have the exclusive licence to sell a certain type of waterproof clothing. You may provide physiotherapy or design large-format murals of cloud-jumping unicorns. Whatever you can do is an Ability. If you are not able to do it, you can't do it, so you can't offer it and so you can't brand it. Abilities have to be your primary focus because nothing happens unless someone is able to do something. So I do always recommend you focus on your central core Abilities, what your brand can actually do, and how that will transform people as a cornerstone to every aspect of your brand's life in the world.

***C stands for Content. This is everything your brand knows;*** and can share with its audiences. Content is a brand's 'material', its Intellectual Property; the stuff a brand tells its audience. A brand leads its audience on a particular path through life's jungle, showing—or telling—that audience what it needs to know. Content is the stories a brand tells its audience and the information, style, voice, and tone it uses to do that. Content is mostly related to a brand's central Abilities, what the brand is actually able to do for the people it serves. What does your brand know?

***T is for Touchpoints. And these are places where your brand touches its audience.*** The channels through which you deliver your Abilities, offerings, and Content.

How will your brand touch people?

Whether a brand sells auto parts, rents out bouncy castles, or analyses zebra crossings, a brand is ultimately composed of Abilities, Content, and Touchpoints.

All successful brands adhere to this same three-armed philosophy. However, every successful brand is different and has a different authentic character and foundation and a different set of unique offerings to bring to the "Conversation of Life". And so each brand will have a different A.C.T. structure, different positioning, different audiences, and a different set of opportunities.

## Give your brand Abilities

Branding is mostly about the framing, and positioning, of what you can do, and offer to people. I.e. your *offerings*.

Which is important because your offerings are the things that your end-users want, the things that actually transform them, the things that keep them coming back for more. These offerings are a direct result of your brand's core Abilities, a result of what it is your brand can do.

If you're a landscape gardener, your Abilities are the landscaping of gardens, and all the ways you can do that—such as the transplanting of saplings, the erecting of fences, and the positioning of concrete cherubs that urinate pump-fed pond water ad infinitum. The quality and perceived quality of these Abilities will be central to your brand's success. It doesn't matter how thick and luxurious your business cards are, or how RUDE your logo is, or how DURABLE your name is if you erect fences that fall over in the lightest breeze, or position cherubs that wee in their own faces, your brand will be thought of as a low-quality brand.

Abilities are key. Without them, your brand cannot go forward.

Abilities should be your number one priority, they are the engine house of your brand. Focus on Abilities first.

If you're a baker and your bread is tasteless, don't spend all your money making a neon sign for your frontage, or writing a series of blog posts about bread. Just make the bread better. Then spend money on signage and Content creation. The best and most successful brands have—at their heart—a really good thing that their audiences just cannot live without.

The 'brand' may well be the gravitational centre that has enabled that special thing into existence—often the desired offerings of a brand come about due to a virtuous cycle between brand and audience which has allowed an 'adjacent possible event'—but it's always important to remember what it is your audience actually values and to steer your priorities to suit those valued things.

---

'These days, people want to learn before they buy,
be educated instead of pitched.'
*Brian Clark*

---

## Give your brand Content

When you're happy your brand's Abilities are in good working order—and you are creating something that you are desperate to let others know about, then, and only then—it is time to start talking.

Content is what your brand knows and it's what your audience wants to know. Content sells. Content creates credibility and trust. This book is Content. I am telling you what I know. I am the author, and so through this work, I am telling you that I am "authorised". And that I have credibility and that you can trust me. At least, that's the hope.

We touched upon Content creation in STEP 8—Give your brand a voice—and looked at how important it is to choose the right things to present and to present them in the right way. There are many tools and techniques available to modern-day Content creators to help them develop their brand's voice and to help them tell stories that draw audiences in, and open people's minds.

> We, humans, are social, conscious beings, travelling what appears to be an open-ended road of existence. We never stop looking for something new to look at, listen to, or interact with. Content provides a steady means of engagement between brand and audience.

Buyers do not like to be sold to, and usually, potential buyers research what it is they want well ahead of any purchase.

Content produced by—or on behalf of—the brand, allows its audience to educate themselves on the latest goods and services and to make better decisions on their own time without the pressure or annoyance of a sales representative up in their personal space. It also means that when the buyer finally gets in front of the seller, less time will be wasted and more quality time can be enjoyed between the brand and its end-user.

We have more means of expression than ever before and more Touchpoint options than we know what to do with ... but when it comes to designing your Content schedule*, the first question you always need to ask is: 'What do we want to say?' and 'why do we want to say it?'

Then—and only then—you can ask 'How should we say it?' and 'How can we deliver this piece of information?' Video? Blog? Advert? Email?

Once you have worked out the message, you can look at the medium.

A good Content schedule* will help you work out where you can best deliver your stories and news to ensure you engage your audience without boring anyone to tears or causing vast numbers to 'unsubscribe'.

You can consider various Content delivery strategies and models, you can use in-app purchases, paywalls, and funnel systems. You can create overture videos, emails, and calls to action that lead people toward landing pages and measure what's working and what's not. Content educates people, and turns your end-users into experts and evangelists. Content gives prospects and decision-makers the answers, justifications, and business cases they need to buy your offerings. Content is a vital bridging point and a valuable sales tool.

* Check out the Give yourself brand 'Content Creator' at **giveyourselfabrand.com/content-creator**

## Give your brand Touchpoints

In today's world, there are many many ways to touch your audiences—apps, advertising, blogs, press, presentations, products, packaging, digital marketing, direct mail, recipe books, point-of-sale, social media, brand ambassadors, celebrity endorsement, Influencers ('YouTubers', 'Instagrammers'), product placement, PR, videos, in-store activations, radio, podcasts, gaming, eLearning, infographics, widgets, stationery, augmented reality, virtual reality, text messages, events, canvas bags, landing pages, outbound comms, inbound comms, SEO, online real estate, email, cross-platform content, paintballing and pop-up beer henges—but what is best for your brand? What will bring you the results you desire?

What is measurable and what would just be a profound waste of budget?

There are many helpful resources online to help you decide but your first stop should be the Give yourself a brand 'Touchpoint Table' to be found by visiting ***giveyourselfabrand.com/touchpoint-tactics***

You may of course require additional Touchpoints more relevant to your offering or industry but this tool—together with your Content creator schedule—will provide a good overview of standard 'general-use' Touchpoint options to get you rolling, so you can start to plan a strategy that uses the right tactics, in the right way, at the right time.

## You need A, C and T to A.C.T. correctly

You need all three—A, C and T—to A.C.T. correctly! And unless you are a super-intelligent Octopus you cannot physically mastermind all three things simultaneously but a good brander can allocate resources wisely and play each off the other. Good Abilities generate good Content which informs good Touchpoints, which can create feedback that can further enhance a brand's Abilities. ACTing can be a virtuous cycle.

Good branding is about blending your Abilities with your Content and delivering everything to your audience via well-considered Touchpoints. It is also about respecting your end-user and that every time your end-user even so much as thinks about your brand, it is a Touchpoint. Your TED Talk is a Touchpoint, but if someone sees you walking into the building, that's also a Touchpoint! That's why your Touchpoints should be authentic. "Keeping up appearances" is easier when your appearances are authentic. Yes, things need thought, editing, and hard work, but life is tricky and many brands need to "grow up in public" so by weaving your A.C.T. "in concert", you become a more congruent and authentic brand.

## Presentation, presentation, presentation

In life, everything is presentation, and presentation is everything.

If you present something right, it will achieve 'buy-in' from your audience, and your audience will 'buy' it. This doesn't necessarily mean you need to present a 24/7 appearance of faultless perfection in expensive hand-crafted designer suits, but if your audience expects expensive suits you should invest in expensive suits, expensive suits the likes of which have never been seen. You could of course completely subvert expectations—there's never been a better time to bring back the shellsuit (Gen Z probably will, if they haven't already ... it's the natural next step after Friends and stone-wash jeans).

But essentially, regardless of your particular generation, the principles that underpin branding are timeless. And a key principle is presentation. And that doesn't mean using smoke and mirrors to hide things, look good, or bamboozle people. It's about selecting that which is best to present and presenting that in the best way possible. So your audience can 'get you'. If your end-users can Observe and Realise the relevance of your work, they can start to ORATE you.

---

'You can have brilliant ideas, but if you can't get them across,
your ideas won't get you anywhere.'
*Lee Iacocca*

---

## Give your audience *Theatre!*

Can you remember what happened the day before your first kiss? Probably not, but I'll bet you remember where you were when you had your first kiss. In branding—as in life—it's the moments that matter.

We all love to be made to feel special.

We never grow out of it.

So take the time, and care, to give that little bit extra, because people appreciate, and remember special moments.

'Hmm' says Uncle Brian, '*Theatre!* sounds expensive.'

Yes, good point, Brian. Adding *Theatre!* to your branding is effective but can be challenging and it's usually a job that requires pleasing two opposing bosses.

One boss is the audience, and the other is your accountant.

And usually what pleases one, infuriates the other.

But over the long term, you need them both to be on your side.

You need to invest in retaining your audience, but you need to balance the books.

'Hang on,' frowns Uncle Brian, 'if you've got a successful product or service, then surely you don't need *Theatre!*'

Well, not everything you do has to be theatrical and 'special'—that could get a little tedious anyway—but if now and then you give your audiences a touch of magic, it goes a long way. Yes, they also like normality, consistency, familiarity, and knowing where things are. Yes, they like process and guidance and "closure"—because we humans like to feel protected and safe within a system to trust it—but once that trust has been won, you need to retain engagement and inspire genuine interest, so your audience can ORATE. Time and time again.

This is the challenge of every brand: to stay consistent in delivering the value for which you are known and staying relevant in changing times. Besides, you always need new business from new fans to provide lifeblood to your business.

And when I say *Theatre!* I don't mean Amateur Dramatics or dressing up as Bottom from A Midsummer Night's Dream. However, if it's true that all the world's a stage then it pays to perform upon that in such a way that gets attention, and for the right reasons.

If your brand sells ride-on lawnmowers, sit on them. Line them up in front of your store. Astroturf your roof. Get your sales team to do some demos. Enter your lawnmowers in your local town's annual carnival as a lawnmower motorcade. Get escorted by a 28-piece brass band playing Born To Be Wild while intermittently firing glitter cannons into the ululating crowds. You'll be remembered. Memorable moments attract people and can guide them through your processes.

*Theatre!* attracts people to the world of your brand—and then sets the stage to touch hearts and minds. People like the personal touch. It shows consideration. Our modern-day world is awash with aloof systems designed to 'blanket bomb' 'prospects' with mind-curdling banality and quite frankly I'm getting a little bored of it.

'It's a numbers game,' scoffs Uncle Brian, 'you've gotta send out a million emails to convert one qualified lead!'

Maybe, but why not add a bit of *Theatre!* instead and watch how the 'numbers game' swings more in your favour. Enliven your customer journeys with relevant yet engaging stories, special moments, and audience participation. It's not necessarily more expensive. It just takes a bit of thought and a bit of courage. Yes, this is non-specific advice, but that's often the best kind of advice. You can add your own spin to it.

---

'People will sit up and take notice of you if you sit up and take notice of what makes them sit up and notice.'
*Harry Gordon Selfridge*

---

## (But use context, timing and some risk)

*Theatre!* is important and magical moments touch people's hearts but knowing when to do something is vital. The success of anything—be it announcements, a compliment, or an impromptu gift—always relies on context and timing. Life is a subtle dance of energies, relationships, and transfers. When to do something is often as important a consideration as what to do. We also need to consider the who, the how, and all the little details that will make the difference between success and failure.

When you buy a birthday gift for someone special the target profile

is very small and manageable. It's just one person to please and cater for. But when you're gifting a large audience of end-users, the task of making everyone feel special and staying on budget, can become overwhelming. So you need to ask yourself some important questions.
What do I want to achieve?
What do I want my audience to think or feel?
What is likely to go wrong or be misread?
Is this too risky? Is this too safe?
Is it a good use of money? Will it make its money back?

You probably won't ever find a perfect solution that ticks all the boxes—every good idea has its negative aspects and unintended consequences—but the more you educate yourself and prepare, the more chance you have of pleasing your crowd.

But there comes a point in any worthwhile project where the road thins out, and you lose your SatNav, and you have to take a risk.

We humans bore quickly and tire of novel trends and so to reach people in new ways often requires bold, new thinking. Bold new thinking that might not work. That is the tension at the heart of every excellent performance we witness. That's the risk every performer takes. You could fall flat on your face, so in pretty much all the best work exists a vulnerability. And audiences like vulnerability, because it's real, and it shows the performer is being brave enough to take a risk, even if that risk has been limited by training and preparation.

Risks should always be limited by training, preparation, and backed up by a good understanding of your audience, and a good sense of timing.

Just because something is good in one scenario doesn't mean it'll work in all scenarios. Glitter is beautiful but glitter is also annoying. In music videos, it can be used to stunning effect but sometimes it's in a greetings card and comes off and goes everywhere, and that's rubbish.

---

'Good timing is invisible.
Bad timing sticks out a mile.'
*Tony Corinda*

---

## Use empathy to create a world for your audience—one they actually want

Every person is—at heart—a wandering spirit looking for refreshment.

Whether you're the weary couple picking out paints, some civil servant searching for steam rooms, the philosopher exploring humanity's purpose, or Barry just looking for a donut, we are all looking for a special space where we can become who we want to be.

We want to go somewhere where everyone knows our name, or somewhere where no one knows our name. Somewhere we can recharge. Some place that ticks our boxes.

And so, for the sake of its end-users' well-being, and sanity, every brand should strive to be a distinctive and desirable geography that can be escaped to, revelled in, and used to meet certain needs.

And when its end-users are safely ensconced inside this world, the host brand—like any good host—has a duty of care to ensure everyone stays happy. There's nothing worse than going to a party you really don't want to go to, and the host forces you to smile for the camera. Make sure the world you create for your end-users is a happy place and not a world of enforced happiness and fake smiles.

The word suggests somewhere physical but a 'world' does not have to be an actual space with GPS coordinates. It can of course be valuable to create a bricks-and-mortar address. Actual locations are absolutely brilliant platforms to extend your brand and create real worlds for your end-user—as any restaurant or theme park owner will confirm—but the actual real estate and physical territories of your world are less important than the idea that exists at the heart of that world. Everything starts with a dream.

---

'You don't need to be a genius or a visionary,
or even a college graduate for that matter.
To be successful, you just need a framework and a dream.'
*Michael Dell*

---

Humans exist in their minds first, before they exist in the real world. And so the ideas in the heads of your end-users—and the feelings in their bodies—are more important than the actual objective spaces they're geographically located in.

To create a world that your end-user desires, you first need to understand them. You need to find out what they want, what they really really want. You need to find the subjective in the objective, the fantasy in the reality. And for this, you will need empathy. Empathy and research.

Both are of key importance.

It takes time, knowledge, and good observation skills, to create desirable worlds. Always remember that people are strange, life is often counter-intuitive, and blind assumption is the mother of all mess-ups. To understand your audience you need a truly empathetic approach, backed up by insights that you find from asking the right questions.

The truly empathic brand doesn't assume anything—the truly empathetic brand always listens to its end-users. It doesn't assume its audience will value what it values. It doesn't assume its audience will notice or care that it's changed the typeface on its website.

A truly empathetic brand tries to see things from its end-user's vantage point.

When considering your authentic ACTivity, you should always put yourself in the shoes of your audience. Whenever the rapper Eminem would finish cutting a track in his state-of-the-art recording studio he would always make a point of recording a copy to a cassette tape before going to play the track in an old car parked out the back of his house. To put himself inside the heads of his fans. To ask himself 'What are they really experiencing?'

When you're devising and realising your ACTivity—and all the detailed planning and logistics and deadlines and problems and brain-shrinking stress—it can become easy to get wrapped up in the production process and snow-blind yourself from the actual people you are hoping to connect with and serve. So, always remember to squeegee your empathy glasses and put yourself in your end-users' shoes.

It is the job of the artist to bring new things into the world and challenge the status quo—so we give special licence to our cultural icons—but there still needs to be a solid grounding point with the audience. Good art is not disconnected and indifferent to reality; good art is radically connected to some vital truth of shared experience. Good artists see the beauty evident in the world and find a way to convey that beauty in a tangible means to an audience.

There's nothing more wince-inducing than an artist completely unconnected from the reality of their fans, bounding onto the stage in ill-considered cheekless leather slacks singing songs that no one likes, 'Put your hands in the air!'

The creation of a desirable, believable, and authentic world is the ultimate work of a brand.

And so, a brand's ACTs should work together in concert to create an ecosystem of interrelated parts that gives its end-users the transformations they seek.

Technology is always changing and new opportunities are emerging everywhere. AI and Virtual- and Augmented-Reality are all fast becoming viable ways of creating profoundly immersive, memorable, and educational, end-user experiences. However, you must have a good rationale and business case for using AI, VR, or AR and any 'trendy' or 'relevant' technology. Otherwise, you may be missing opportunities for your audience to better ORATE your brand.

It is said that 'buyers require seven points of contact' before they trust a brand enough to proceed with an order. Having an accessible world of Content available for prospective end-users, from a wide range of sources, like wiki pages, external reviews, webpages, social media platforms, and video content, is vital to credentialise and back up your offerings. And because your brand now exists on such a strong platform, you will be well placed to start attracting social proof that can show any interested party your brand is a credible 'world' worth visiting.

I have thrown about eighteen metric tonnes of paper-based direct mail into my recycling bin, and have worn my fingers to the bone unsubscribing from inane email blasts, and I'm sure I'm not alone.

Yes, I know it's a "numbers game", Brian, and no, you can't please all the people all the time, and sometimes an indiscriminate campaign of "door-drops" might just pay for itself but your first objective must always be to truly empathise with your audience.

To get big in Japan, or Ashby-de-la-Zouch, you must create better conditions for connection and growth and make your budgets go further. Consider better what you're offering, how you can convey that, and who you're talking to.

## (and your world must be accessible and available)

You need to be available to your audience and so you must site and position your brand's world appropriately. In your work in STEP 3 (Give yourself an end-user) you did some thinking as to where your end-user hangs out—use this to plan and check how accessible your 'world' is. And remember, a brand's world can be divided into two parts, Offerings and Signposts:

1). Offerings: your brand's actual 'world'. By which I mean the actual work, or rather the things you offer to end-users and the places where your offerings transform them.

2). Signposts: The content and touchpoints that signpost end-users to your brand's 'world' i.e. the marketing, promotions, invitations, and the wider world of demand generation.

Imagine your brand is set up to teach people how to code (to become programmers). Let's name this fictitious brand CodeTrip. Any banner adverts or press articles written about CodeTrip are part of its 'Signposting', they are helpful beacons that can signpost people towards CodeTrip's actual 'Offerings'—e.g. its website, training sessions, or eLearning apps—where you engage directly with your end-users. Seeing your brand as a world like this can help you ensure your end-users can find and access your brand when they need to.

And ensure all the "entry points" are in good working order.

People have little time to wait around. If your website takes over two seconds to load, you'll lose people. If your links are broken, you'll lose people. If your shop is closed, guess what, you'll lose people.

It is very easy to lose people.

If people want to find—and engage with—your world, you must ensure they can.

## Create a brandscape

A brand's ultimate goal is to create a 'world' for its audience, but building a world can take a long time, so where do you begin? In the first instance, look to create a 'brandscape'. Your world can become bigger, deeper, wider, and more mature with time, but initially think of your brand as a new garden people can visit.

Initially, your garden might look a little underloved and there's little point denying it. You may look a little vulnerable, but remember: vulnerability breeds connection.

In the beginning, your brand may not have many followers, videos, or people talking about you online. But if you put the important things in place—Ability, good Content and engaging Touchpoints: e.g. a good online presence, videos and emails—you create a brandscape on which to start building upwards. Choose ACTivity that best suits your brand's foundation, its offerings, and its end-users.

Visit ***giveyourselfabrand.com/touchpoint-tactics*** to help you work out which parts would best suit your brand, to begin with.

Position your brandscape to be available, convenient, and accessible. Use your knowledge and feelings of your end-user to judge the best geographical and/or online locations to best suit your Offerings or Signposts. The more you know your end-user, the more intelligent and efficient your brandscape can be.

It's important to set up a world i.e. a 'place and space' for your audience, and the wider your world is, the more fans you can attract but you can't be everywhere. And certainly not in the initial phases. So don't waste time setting up 'real estate' that probably won't be visited—e.g. choose the most appropriate locations and social media platforms, the ones your end-users actually use.

A 'brandscape' should have at its core, a set of 'touchstones'* that serve as 'gravitational centres' for the brand. If you have a physical HQ—or flagship store—this will be key among your touchstones. However, if you don't have a physical focal point, your brandscape should feature a central website for all top-level reference and mailing list generation.

Focus first on establishing this core to your brandscape, before you start growing anything else. It's better to have one or two strong Touchpoints, than fifty weak ones.

* 'Touchstones' are essentially Super Touchpoints.

## Give your brand reach

Your brand needs to reach people.

Your brand needs "reach".

If your fans are to ORATE you, and your offerings, you need to get that O pumped up ... you need to be Observed.

But that's not as easy as it sounds.

You've got a big potential fan base out there in the wider world but...

...the wider world is big, and people are busy, and creatures of habit, established markets are saturated, advertising is expensive, your budget may be very tight right now, and anyway, most people simply ignore adverts.

Now, before you get too depressed, remember that you don't need to be big the world over, and you don't even need to be big in Japan, you just need to be big enough, initially, to cover your running costs and maintain a Minimal Viable Product.

Besides, even though you're rightly proud of what you've achieved so far, and your brand looks amazing to you, it won't be perfect and there will be certain things that need improvement.

And that's ok.

When you start out playing the guitar you don't use huge amplifiers turned towards massive crowds, exaggerating every shortcoming you have.

Provided you box clever, and know your audience, and remember the MAPPPA* principle, and have trust in your brand's new foundation, you can proceed to ACT and attain reach in a natural way.

Trust your Abilities, create good Content, build strong Touchpoints. Choose good platforms. Optimise your website. Build your mailing lists. Make videos, or let the public make your videos for you (fan-generated). Good ideas get shared. Yes, I'm looking at you, Cadbury's gorilla.

You can, of course, pay cash money for "reach"—advertising, PR and marketing, inbound and outbound comms, etc.—but the most valuable and cost-effective reach is 'organic reach' created when people share your stuff for free (just because they want to!). There's no magic formula to creating this 'viral wonderstuff' but knowing what, when, and where, to A.C.T. certainly helps.

* Motivation. Approval. Patience. Preparation. Peace. Appreciation. (It's the future!)

## What, when and where to A.C.T.?

Knowing where and when to A.C.T. is key in the building of your brand. You may be limited as to where you can perform your Abilities. If for example, you are a kiln-based pottery or a rack-based cloud storage provider you need a locked-down physical location, and can't be travelling your kilns and racks willy-nilly from town to town in a customised tour bus. You could be a freelance web designer working throughout Europe, a sales coach with multiple bases in the US, or a personal stylist. You could be a make-up artist with no clients, overwhelmed at the choice of promotional options, unsure where to invest your time, and becoming flustered at not knowing where to start. Knowing where and when to partake in your Abilities, and where and when to share your Content and touch end-users via Touchpoints can be a dilemma.

The key is to stay calm, start small, and prioritise accordingly.

Take comfort in the fact that you have built a strong brand foundation, and you can now use the information you created in that process to help you:

– Create an ***Ability Audit*** to seek out and capture all the amazing skills and all that hidden power you have in your life. It's a sad fact that people so often forget what they're good at, and where they've had glimmerings of real success, simply because the pace of life forces most to drop anything that doesn't make immediate money. If it's true that our lives are '99% invisible' then now is the time to shine a light on those bits we had to file away for 'someday'. Make today that day and download your pdf worksheet waiting for you at: ***giveyourselfabrand.com/findyourwhy***

– Create a ***Content Creator*** —a schedule to help you keep on top of all your Content ideas, and ensure they get developed and optimised. To learn more simply visit: ***giveyourselfabrand.com/content-creator***

– Create a ***Touchpoint strategy***, to help you choose Touchpoints that will actually work and that will attract and retain end-users.

There are millions of ways to touch your end-user but to help get you started with some standard practices, visit:
***giveyourselfabrand.com/touchpoint-tactics***

The work of building your brand's world and signposting people to it is never-ending but using the above tips and resources should help you get your ducks in order and help you use every part of the cow, so you avoid wasting time and effort on things that probably won't serve you that much.

Branding is supposed to be fun, so get the above points nailed down, then concentrate on enjoying the process of giving your brand a life.

## Let's get physical

In the good old days, if we wanted a new watch, we'd either get taken out on our father's yacht for a spot of sea-fishing and on the homeward leg be presented with his Philippe Patek Grand Complication, or, in my case, we'd go to the high street jeweller with a Cornish pasty and lovingly fingermark the Perspex cabinets, before seeing if we could get it cheaper in Argos. (And maybe borrow a little blue pen.)

But nowadays we just spend twenty minutes on Amazon and a day or two later we check behind the flowerpot to see what the delivery fairies have left. This new way of doing things is of course both a blessing and a curse.

On the one hand, we feel happy we got our edible candy jockstrap without incident or injury but on the other, we feel lesser for it, robbed of adventure and anecdotes and hollow inside. ('Did I tell you about the time I received a package at my house? Oh, ok bye.')

It's also a double-edged sword for the retailer.

They don't have to pay the expensive rent or rates of a high street store and can streamline their operation to shave expenses and amplify revenues, ***however***, they lose a vital connection point and potentially reduce their ability to touch their audience—an increasingly twitchy and apathetic audience who are making informed yet indifferent consumer decisions online, in their pyjamas, in a cloud of cinnamon vape, via screens, that can only show pictures and videos and words.

As our world becomes ever more digital we find we have less to hold on to and less physical connection between brand and end-user.

Sure, if you're selling edible candy jockstraps, you probably want less physical interaction with your end-users—as these are often low-frequency purchases rather than everyday essentials—but if you're selling high-frequency goods and services like toilet paper, nutritional supplements, shoes, training programs, pilates, apps or any goods or services where greater end-user loyalty could translate to a long-term high-value revenue stream, it's worth touching people where it counts.

People love that which is tangible, proximate, recent, and that which touches them in a meaningful way, and leaves an impression on their senses and memory banks. If your offering just turns up in a generic—and instantly discarded—cardboard box, the only Touchpoint is the offering itself. And no one wants a branded flyer in that box, or a set of car stickers, so the offering itself (whatever it is) becomes your one means of audience connection, and so that'd better be good. And even if it is good, it comes to the end-user in the same way as many other products, and so in this growing culture of online-only engagement, brand potency can get weak and diluted.

It pays to constantly consider how people can physically engage with your brand, so you can make an impression and prolong the connection in a meaningful way, wherever you can. It's not easy. People are forgetful, capricious and always moving forward in a world of distraction—the "Porthole of Now". Things that are on our radars right now get our attention, we're focused on the immediate and what's happening next. Once something's gone, it's gone. Done with. (I believe it's known as 'recency bias'.) Things done last year, last month, and last week are ancient history. Unless they shook or impressed us. And even then your short-term memory records over those impressions without a second thought. The launch event was amazing when it happened but that amazement can dissolve like a Scotch mist. You check your email inbox and there seems to be an inbox error—where are the inquiries from all those interested people you spoke to? Why isn't your brand on the news?

Because your brand is now *yesterday's* news; the branded pen got left on the train and your brochure is in the recycling bin. People are moving on with their lives. If you really want to touch your audiences, you have to do it at source, when you have the opportunity. Make the moment count. Reinvest your event budget, don't spend on branded water bottles—unless your event is in a desert. Instead, put that budget into a unicycling firebreather or something that will leave an impression on the day.

Give away free cameras, or something fun and useful and ideally relevant to the event. Just because your rivals give away boiled sweets or branded vuvuzelas doesn't mean you should. Break the mould. Stand out. Put yourself in your end-users' shoes (Eminem-style) and give away Touchpoints that mean something.

Touch with meaning.

Whether that's event-based widgets, or interactions in-store with 'organic reach' via social media. It's worth spending the time to consider how best you can connect physically. It's better you leave one good impression than a hundred forgotten ones.

And ask yourself 'What do I want to be remembered for?'

People are emotionally connected to that which is proximate but absence makes the heart grow stronger, and scarcity increases value.

If you act out of desperation or confusion, you just create Touchpoints that convey desperation and confusion.

If you source the cheapest T-shirts and flashlights so you can 'touch' more people, you're just showing more people how cheap your brand is. If the stitching of your garments comes loose in your end-user's hand, the stitching of your brand comes loose in that end-user's mind. Everything is association.

Position and presentation influence perception.

Invest in touching your end-users in ways that convey the spirit and values of your brand.

---

'Luxury must remain invisible. But it must be felt.'
*Coco Chanel*

---

## Give your audience stories

Stories show us meaningful patterns. Where before we saw only meaningless data, we now see reason and relevance. Stories educate, entertain, and inspire.

Everyone loves a good story. But why?

Because good stories are brilliant teachers. They transform people. Transform consciousness. You were thinking this way, and now you are thinking that way.

Stories are the most powerful thing in the universe—apart from maybe love, or the energy of stars, or maybe some race of really powerful alien.

But what is a story anyway? And how would you describe one to an alien, if one were to ask, 'What is this thing you humans call "Story?"'

You could say a story was:

– a retelling of happenstance.

– information regarding an event or set of events introduced, sequenced and disclosed in such a way as to create a meaningful narrative arc with a beginning, a middle, and an end.

– a neat packet of ordered information that educates, surprises, delights, and entertains.

Stories take many forms. They can be told to us at bedtime, pitched over a market stall, or projected onto the silver screen but ultimately they are simply the answer to the questions: 'What happened and why?'

Anything can happen. A man could lose his car keys, visit Mars, or hunt a shark. A girl could find some porridge, overcome a bully, or visit her grandmother in the deep dark woods. A bear could attack a village, help a young mancub, or arrive at Paddington station with a marmalade sandwich.

All stories serve the same role: to convey information in a way that makes the information stickier and more memorable to the audience. Jaws could have been conveyed as a series of pie charts but it wouldn't have been as captivating or memorable.

Stories transfix us, transport us, and transform us. They captivate an audience that just wants to know: 'Now what? Now what? Now what?' Stories allow us to captivate our audience to make information memorable. If you can effectively make stories come alive time and time again, in your Abilities, Content, and Touchpoints your brand *will* live happily ever after.

---

'We tell ourselves stories in order to live.'
*Joan Didion*

---

'The engineers of the future will be poets.'
*Terence McKenna*

---

## (and remember to share your failures)

There's nothing more boring than having to listen to someone recount their successes—unless, of course, the successes were achieved at the end of a long line of failures. Why is this?

Because the greater the opposition a protagonist has in a story, the greater the narrative arc. It's why we all love the 'underdog'—the underdog has the biggest mountain to climb and therefore the greater story to tell.

A story is how a hero overcomes challenges and how they are transformed as a result. If nothing goes wrong, there's no story.

Failure, and how you overcome failure, is the foundation of storytelling. And failure is the cornerstone of comedy. And comedy—well, good comedy that makes you laugh—is a very effective means of engaging with audiences and delivering compelling information in a way that makes it compelling and memorable. So talk about your failures. Problems are the fuel of stories. Where there's a problem, there's usually a joke.

Some say 'comedy is tragedy plus time' but I think it's better to say 'comedy is tragedy plus distance' i.e. it's funny as long as it happens to someone else. When the tragedy is distanced from you, when someone else falls over—or makes a gaff—it's funny, but when it happens to you, it isn't.

For a while anyway. But with the distance of time, you can begin to see the funny side of your own mishap, when you become someone else in a sense.

Many would naturally be concerned that sharing their failures may make them sound amateurish or unprofessional. A car resprayer may have had a terrible day and accidentally sprayed a whole fleet of cars the wrong colour, doing thousands of pounds of damage. 'I'm not sharing that story!' they may think, because while it could be very funny to the people not involved (at a distance), it could be job-threatening to those that are. If you were thinking of using this company to spray your car, you might think again after hearing this story. It's a very real and potentially expensive error of judgment to disclose this event if no one else knows about it. A scandal. Then again, it could be the best thing you ever did. If you used it to bring attention to a problem in your core Abilities, a problem that you've now fixed which resulted in an unseen benefit for the end-user, then such a story could be gold dust. Failures make good stories. Vulnerability breeds connection, remember.

Obviously, a story needs to be well told to engage an audience, but the authentic details it hangs on usually need to be based on real-life events, the things you couldn't make up if you tried.

Great stories, well told, get shared.

Some formats are more shareable than others. This will depend on your audience but videos—or links to videos—on channels like YouTube are more likely to be viewed and shared on social media than a link to a written blog or podcast. When a story is good and made shareable it can achieve greater organic reach and even "go viral".

Sharing your failures could be the best decision you ever made.

The famous chandelier scene in the hit comedy Only Fools And Horses was based on an actual job that the writer's father was on. The writer, John Sullivan, asked if he could use this true story and his father said 'No!' It was, after all, a serious matter and people he knew had lost their jobs over the cock-up. But thankfully, John wrote it anyway and made comedy gold. And apparently, his father forgave him and found it very funny on-screen. (If you haven't seen it, YouTube: 'Del and Rodney Smash the Chandelier'.)

'Brace yourself, Rodney, brace yourself.'

---

'Storytelling is the most powerful way
to put ideas into the world today.'
*Robert McAfee Brown*

---

## The stories have to be truthful, right?

It is the job of the raconteur to engage the audience and capture imaginations, however in brand messaging and marketing when you are representing—and making claims about—products and services, you should proceed with caution.

We are told to 'never let the truth get in the way of a good story', but if you lead people to actually believe false information about your offering, you could be falling foul of the Trade Descriptions Act and may find yourself at risk of criminal prosecution.

You must give your audience the information it needs to distinguish between hype and reality. Even if that's done in the small print.

This is why so many brand Touchpoints such as adverts and product packages come with footnotes and disclaimers declaring where the visual representation shown *differs* from the actual offering—for example, many television spots for gaming products feature an exhilarating soundtracked montage sequence alongside a disclaimer saying: 'Not actual gameplay'.

Another potential conflict to consider in brand storytelling is the tension between engagement and trust.

Considering the best stories maintain audience engagement by employing maximum *misdirection*, it's no real surprise that Ian Fleming—the prolific and successful storyteller who brought us the world of James Bond—started his working life devising espionage operations during World War Two, concocting narratives to misdirect the enemy.

The storyteller is an illusionist who has to stay ahead of her audience, feeding it red herrings, while she prepares a storyline that deviates from the expected one. A new reality that can be revealed at a key moment for maximum punch.

This is essentially the same way a joke works. All jokes are mini-stories, where a certain "reality" is established—via a set-up—and the punchline shows you an unexpected series of events, usually culminating in a twist at the end. 'Oh, you thought it would be like that, didn't you? Well, it's gonna be like this!' shock, gasp, applause. But while the unexpected reality is a surprise, it still has to make sense, and relate to the set-up—that's the rule of comedy.

That's the lightbulb moment.

The spark of recognition detonates the laugh.

For example 'Two birds are on a perch ... one says 'you smell fish"? The first five words set up an expectation i.e. they suggest a reality where two birds are on a typical wooden perch, and the last five words shatter that reality, confirming that the birds are actually in fact on a fish, a fish called a perch. The joke hangs on the fact that the word 'perch' has two meanings.

That's joke-writing 101, and it shares the same basic principle of good storytelling. Set up a reality, and then serve up an unexpected storyline or punchline that also makes sense.

But here we have our tension or conflict...

...on the one hand, branding is all about engaging and building up trust with your audience through being authentic and 'transparent' and telling good stories, and on the other, good storytelling is about misdirection and deceiving your audience.

So how do you build up trust while effectively lying to your audience?

Or rather, how do you tell a good story about your brand, without leading your audience to believe something false?

Firstly, you have a duty of care to ensure your audience has a good grasp of the context in which you are presenting your Touchpoints and delivering your Content. Your end-user should always know the "rules of engagement" so to speak.

Your brand should ensure the Touchpoint it is using to tell the "story" (whatever that is) does indeed adhere to the laws, codes, and regulations that govern that particular Touchpoint.

For example, films can only be released to the public after they've been certificated, and advertisers are at risk of censorship, or prosecution if their adverts breach advertising standards. Regulations vary depending on the Touchpoint and the territory.

Secondly, your brand has to win the trust of your audience, and build up a rapport, so it can earn sufficient engagement to use greater artistic licence, and ultimately tell better stories.

The storyteller can bring much to the table, but the strength of the story will determine the level to which it touches people.

Tell stories so good your audience can't ignore them.

Tell stories so good your audience learns something truthful about your brand.

Tell stories so good your audience finds consolation, answers to their existential problems, fellowship, escape, and hope.

Stories can be a difficult sell in the boardroom. Unless sold well, the idea of "story", and narrative, is often ignored in quarterly meetings and not seen as a worthy topic for discussion.

'Right,' frowns Uncle Brian, suitcase in hand as he chomps the last of his pre-commute Jaffa cake, 'because stories aren't real.'

Ok, Brian, sure. Narratives are rightly mistrusted and left at the door of many boardrooms in favour of P&L ledgers, trading forecasts, and strategic growth initiatives. And often, stories are hard to analyse, and/or verify, but truth be told, stories do in fact drive markets and influence customer decisions and, when all is said and done, stories are the only things that ever really endure.

---

'People do not buy goods and services, they buy relations,
stories and magic.'
*Seth Godin*

---

## Addressing the 'end' problem of 'Brand Storytelling'

'Brand Storytelling' has been a popular phrase in recent years, however, it is a confusing phrase—what does it mean? Does it mean we should develop our whole brand as if it were just one story? Because this creates a problem: a good story needs a good ending, but you don't want to 'end' your brand. That would be brand suicide. So what, pray tell, is the answer?

The trick is to treat your brand as one character in a series of stories, rather than driving your brand into a narrative cul-de-sac. That way you can be a great storyteller, produce a constant turnover of Content, and make your brand a hero. Simples.

> See your brand as the central character in your stories. By serving things up as digestible adventures, you keep people interested with beginnings, middles, and ends, and you can show the valuable lessons your brand learns along the way (a key feature of any good story).

This doesn't mean you have to personify your brand with an actual person or brand mascot—although that can be helpful (see overleaf). But because a brand is all about long-term engagement: it must keep its audience engaged in an ever-changing world. And yet it must all the while stay the same, so as not to lose its audience. If a brand chooses to live its life like a character in a story—like a James Bond, like a Zoe Washburne, or a Donald Duck—it can keep its audience enraptured forever.

The external world—the one you share with your audience—is the backdrop to your adventures, ensuring your brand stays relevant and up-to-date. You can still provide your end-user with pure escapism—with a fantasy world—but 'fantasy' worlds that connect somewhere with the real world, are the most effective. Look at Harry Potter, Star Wars, and The Lord of the Rings. Look at any enduring work of fantasy fiction, and see how it says something about the real world, about values, about how to live. Stories are tools, here to help us work out problems and to transform us from one state to another, inside a sense of identity.

## Consider 'mascots' to personify your brand

Mascots as metaphors can provide you with an effective way of presenting your brand's unique selling points. After all, the most important, interesting—and endlessly fascinating thing to people—is people. We are social beings, so using people or personified characters (often called personas) can help your audience relate to your brand.

Mascots can either stand centre stage as the 'face' of your brand, or they can act in a supporting role, like a side-kick—(Uncle Brian, for example) a valuable role that can represent the thoughts of the audience and ask any necessary questions.

Mascots are great for aiding exposition, and by which I mean: they can explain what's going on.

'How many hours does this battery last for? Seventeen! Wow! That's 50% longer than any other battery!'

Not only do memorable characters help your brand get ORATE'd but they can also improve brand recognition. Just look at some famous brand mascots used in advertising over the last hundred years:

- The Meerkats of Meerkovo *(Compare the Market)*
- The Milky Bar kid *(Milky Bar)*
- The Duracell Bunnies *(Duracell)*
- The Nescafe couple *(Nescafe)*
- The Smash alien robots *(Smash)*
- The Michelin Man *(Michelin)*
- Mickey Mouse *(Disney)*
- Tony the Tiger (*Kellogg's Frosties)*
- Coco the Monkey *(Kellogg's Cocopops)*
- Captain Morgan *(Captain Morgan)*
- Red and Yellow *(M&M's)*
- Animal *(Peperami)*
- Bertie Bassett *(Liquorice Allsorts)*

As these examples show, 'mascots' can be quite 'left-field'—they needn't be too 'obvious'. But ensure they grow out of a central truth so they retain a certain relevance and authenticity. And if you do need to show any nudity ensure it is strictly necessary to the plot.

'If you want to build a ship, don't drum up people to collect wood and don't assign them tasks and work, but rather teach them to long for the endless immensity of the sea.'
*Antoine de Saint-Exupéry*

## Always make your brand the hero

Stories can be the lifeblood of a brand. Once a brand's foundation has been laid—and once its Abilities are in full working order—it needs to constantly change things up without essentially changing itself. It must engage audiences while staying the same, and it must stay the same without being predictable...

> 'Hang on,' coughs Uncle Brian, 'but I reckon you're overthinking this! If you're a petrol company and sell petrol through service stations, just put your service stations near busy roads and make sure the fuel pumps work. Don't worry too much about stories!'
>
> Ok, fine, I hear you. If you are creating a brand that sells petrol—or similar—then sure, you will need to address a massive range of logistical considerations. But those logistical considerations fall under the category of Abilities, which, as I have said, are not within my remit. My purview is to demonstrate where branding can help you leverage your abilities. I'm not saying storytelling is *all* you need to make a brand. Ok?
>
> 'Sure.'
>
> Oh, and Brian ... just one last thing. Look at humanity, look at history, look at the way we make sense of our lives. It's all just story. Religion, commerce, consumerism, education, science, politics, art, and culture. Everything is just an arrangement of narratives. But whatever techniques and devices you use to tell your stories, always remember that ultimately, it's your brand that's the hero.

The hero who fights battles and overcomes challenges to bring their audience the answers and tools they need to lead better lives. Heinz is a hero for bringing us a tomato ketchup that takes its time. Nike is a hero for giving us great sportswear and inspiring us by being a positive presence in the world. Apple is a hero for enabling us to think different, create, communicate, and connect. Google is a hero for giving us a lightning-fast internet search engine. Starbucks is a hero for providing somewhere to meet others, relax, and work. And Marmite is a hero (to half the population) for bringing us its yeast extract. Whatever your brand's stories, whatever your brand's character, whatever your recurring themes, battles, and overarching quests—your aim should be to make your brand a hero that makes the world a better place.

**A hero with a super Why**
**A hero with a values-driven Ethos**
**A hero with a defined End-user**
**A hero with a DURABLE Name**
**A hero with a DURABLE Line**
**A hero with a RUDE Identity**
**A hero with a DAPPER Style**
**And a hero with a DAPPER Voice**

## Keep on truckin'

Whoa! You've reached the last double-page spread.

You've completed this book and (if you followed all the steps) you now have a very strong brand foundation.

But the work is not over.

In fact, it has only just begun...

...because branding is about long-term engagement.

Whatever new thing you add, is going to need curating for a long time. And it's therefore important that you manage that.

I was stuck in a traffic jam a while back and planted in the same spot of road—outside a well-known home improvement centre—for half an hour. The only thing I had to entertain myself was a lovely hedge to my right. It didn't do much by way of entertaining, after all, it was only a hedge, but I appreciated the way the light caught its leaves and spider webs. And then I noticed it was actually overgrown by about thirty per cent. I saw this because I noticed behind the hedge was a sign for the very home improvement centre that owned the overgrown hedge.

I squinted through the leaves to see a picture of a member of staff doing a thumbs up and next to him the words 'Come in and meet Dave, our new carpentry expert!'

'Blimey,' I thought, 'never mind carpentry, has this brand heard of hedge trimmers? They probably *sell* hedge trimmers! Dave could probably come out and trim the hedge himself!'

This one innocent hedge created a powerful "disconnect" between the brand and its audience (in this case, me).

Maintain your storefronts and "shop windows". You have to show up and show you're ready to serve and that it's "business as usual".

Another time, I was online—planning how to entertain my children over a fast-approaching bank holiday weekend—and I found a website for a local(ish) family-friendly wildlife centre. The home page featured a garish advert inviting me to 'Come and see Denzil, our 900 lb saltwater crocodile!' He was obviously their star attraction because he featured on every page of the website. Every page. Large pictures of him crowbarred into the content. A bit unfair on all the other animals at the park but hey, given my son's love of big reptiles I was completely sold, and I made my way to the 'How to find us page'. Scrolling down, at the bottom of the page was a tiny message written in sombre grey type: 'In memory of Denzil, who sadly died two years ago'.

Now, I'm as chilled out as the next man, and understand that such mistakes happen, of course they do, and that's ok—I am in no position to judge, having made hundreds of similar errors throughout my life but ... could it be time for some website updates?

I guess my point here is this: you need to maintain things, every minute of every day. And *that* is not easy.

Distractions are everywhere, we can only do one thing at a time and other tasks are always screaming for our attention...

...but you need to put priorities and systems in place to ensure you lubricate the things that need to keep rolling and waste less time on lesser wheels just because they squeak louder.

That's the trick. The main trick of branding is to stay relevant and consistent in an ever-changing world. The world *does* change—hedges grow, domain names expire, crocs pass on—but you must maintain consistency of service. You must tread water and make it look effortless, despite the crocodiles.

At the start that is easy, but as time goes by, it becomes harder. So you must be prepared to *sustain* your ACTivity and that's why it's so important to do things you love and follow your heart because the work of branding is hard work. A brand must keep people's attention, while essentially staying the same. It must earn trust and it must earn engagement.

For a brand to be successful it must serve its short-term needs without compromising too much on its higher goals. And vice versa.

It must make enough profit to survive while adhering to a values system that makes it all worthwhile. For a brand to be successful, it must serve its own needs and those of its audience. It must be self-centred and empathetic. It must lead and it must follow. For a brand to be successful, it must transform and stay consistent, it must change with the times to stay fresh and relevant in this world while ostensibly staying the same to retain its audiences. In short, for a brand to be a heaven for its end-users, it must do a hell of a lot.

So take all this advice, find what works for you, and keep on truckin'.

And that's the end of this book. You made it. Well done.

Now the hard work begins.

This is where you sparkle.

**'Knowledge is of no value unless you put it into practice.'**

*Anton Chekhov*

**'You must be the change you wish to see in the world.'**

*Mahatma Gandhi*

**'The distance is nothing; it's only the first step that is difficult.'**

*Marquise Du Deffand*

**Learn more at:
giveyourselfabrand.com**

www.ingramcontent.com/pod-product-compliance
Lightning Source LLC
LaVergne TN
LVHW091303150826
845673LV00006B/1524
*9781916017092*